*Oz.... ... .......*
*Stereotype and Reality*
Tom Koob with Curtis Copeland

# Ozarks Hillbilly

Copyright © 2021 Tom Koob and Curtis Copeland

ISBN# 978-1-7923-7141-7

WHITE OAK LODGE PUBLISHING

24039 Box Elder
Shell Knob, MO. 65747

Printed in the United States of America
Litho Printers & Bindery
Cassville, Missouri 65625

"Tom Koob and Curtis Copeland serve as guides on a tour of the Ozarks of legend and reality. *Ozarks Hillbilly* introduces readers to examples of hillbilly stereotypes from generations of writers, but Koob and Copeland also combat the stereotypes through the stories of real-life Ozarkers. It's a useful approach that makes this a valuable book for students of the region's history and mythology."
—Dr. Brooks Blevins, Noel Boyd Professor of Ozarks Studies at Missouri State University

"It's amazing! I love the tone, flow, continuity, everything! It's like a doctoral thesis that is engaging and accessible to everyone! Great job, youns!
—Angel Wolf, great-granddaughter of Mary Elizabeth Mahnkey

"Tom Koob and Curtis Copeland bring together sources in an interesting way that helps the reader understand the caricature and the reality of Ozarkers. And it's a great resource for other writers who may want to create Ozark stories while remaining true to our culture."
—Hayden Head, PhD, professor emeritus, College of the Ozarks

"*Ozarks Hillbilly* goes far beyond its description as a study of stereotypes. As a flatlander from Kansas who arrived 48 years ago, this book helps me understand my personal journey into the culture of the Ozarks over time.

This is a deep dive into what is now a part of my history, told in the voices of both natives and outsiders who visited and stayed. For natives it provides unexpected historical insights. It should be required reading for new arrivals to what is now 'our' land."
—Barbara and Bob Kipfer, Master Naturalists and conservationists

# Acknowledgements

This book originated from a discussion the authors had regarding Billy Redden, the "banjo boy" from the movie *Deliverance*. Curtis Copeland's experience with Billy is told in the Introduction. This discussion confirmed the authors' belief that the stereotypical view of the Ozarks hillbilly was uninformed and unfair at best and insulting and damaging at worst. The authors combined their interests, researched the existing literature on the subject and then collaborated to produce this book that they hope provides a new perspective on the duality of the term "hillbilly."

Many people helped us along the way. Writers and researchers in the academic world were instrumental in providing thorough and documented data regarding the origins, development and uses of the hillbilly epithet and its duality. Dr. Brooks Blevins, the Noel Boyd Professor of Ozarks Studies at Missouri State University, was supportive and we relied heavily on his body of work, including *Arkansas/Arkansaw How Bear Hunters, Hillbillies and Good Ol' Boys Defined a State, Hill Folks A History of Arkansas Ozarkers & Their Image* and *Ghost of the Ozarks Murder and Memory in the Upland South*. Dr. Blake Perkins, Chair of the Department of History and Political Science at Williams Baptist University, provided encouragement and definitive information in his doctoral dissertation, *Dynamics of Defiance: Government Power and Rural Resistance in the Arkansas Ozarks* and his book *Hillbilly Hellraisers Federal Power and Populist Defiance in the Ozarks*. We gleaned useful information from Archie Green's comprehensive 1965 *Hillbilly Music: Source and Symbol* and J.W. Williamson's *Hillbillyland*.

We relied on the early chroniclers Henry Rowe Schoolcraft, Frederick Gerstaecker, George W. Featherstonhaugh and Father John Joseph Hogan to reveal the early outlanders' view of the Ozarks inhabitants. The developing stereotyped image was fleshed out in the writings of the Southwestern humorists Charles Noland, Thomas Thorpe, Albert Pike and Opie Read. More realistic and sometimes romanticized accounts were supplied by Silas Turnbo and Harold Bell Wright. We value the much more positive and complimentary writing of true Ozarkers like Mary Elizabeth Mahnkey, Douglas Mahnkey and May Kennedy McCord. We are indebted to the extensive and comprehensive bodies of work laid down by Vance Randolph and Otto Rayburn. Their long-term study and documentation of all things Ozarkian is a treasure trove of information for amateur researchers like us. Fictional books by Charlie May Simon, Donald Harington and Thames Williamson provided unique, talented perspectives. More recent work by Ellen Gray Massey and Phyllis Rossiter brought us a realistic, complimentary view of the Ozarks hillbilly.

The authors have included images that we hope illustrate our objective and highlight both the negative and positive representations that have been portrayed. We think the quality of the Randolph photos used with permission of the Lyons Memorial Library and the Godsey photos used with permission of the Godsey Photography Foundation are particularly stunning and honest. The Branson Centennial Museum and the Barry County Museum were gracious in providing both research leads and photographs.

At the risk of leaving someone out, we would like to thank all the writers, reviewers, librarians, friends and family members who helped us with this project. Most of all, we want to recognize and thank the individuals who shared with us their personal stories. It is these individual and family accounts that really bring both our book and its premise to life. Getting to know these folks has allowed us to recognize and appreciate the true image of the Ozarks hillbilly.

# Table of Contents

# Introduction

*Hillbilly*. The word sounds rather simple; an amusing, rhyming colloquialism. But when attempting to describe the word "hillbilly," its concept, its meaning, as completely as possible, it is really rather complex. Being labeled a "hillbilly" may be a badge of honor, or it may be a scathing insult, depending upon the situation, as well as the individual making the designation. When one is called a "hillbilly" as an insult from a friend, it is frequently accepted as a light-hearted joke, usually followed by a laughing acceptance or an equally pointed rebuttal of the same. On the other hand, to be called a "hillbilly" as a compliment from an outsider, or outlander, is nearly as bad as being referred to as a "hillbilly" in a derogatory fashion…it seems bogus and uninformed, even conceited and patronizing.

The term "hillbilly" is used across the United States in both rural and urban settings and has become somewhat common in our modern language. As we journey through this book, we will find that the term has its origins in Europe from centuries ago. Characterizations of the hillbilly are commonly associated with Appalachia and other rural areas of North America. But the focus of this book is on the "Ozarks Hillbilly."

In the grand scheme of things, the Ozarks hillbilly image that most likely comes to the mind of people, especially those outside of the Ozarks, is a relatively new concept. In this book, we will find that the common "Ozarks Hillbilly Image" was actually "created," perpetuated, and promoted in the twentieth century, often for financial gain. We will also find that the long-time resident and generational Ozarkers did not refer to themselves as hillbillies nor was the term commonly used by them until well into the twentieth century. Although many Ozarkers today embrace the idea of being called a hillbilly, and utilize it as a source of regional pride, they are very familiar with the negative connotations of the term and are quick to defend what it means to be a real Ozarks hillbilly.

"Hillbilly", like many words in our English language, especially those words associated so closely with a specific culture, are in a state of metamorphosis. Cultures, terms, and words that are not fully understood are sometimes altered in status or degraded to a term of insult or derogation. The Ozarks hillbilly stereotype, especially as perceived by those outside of the Ozarks region itself, is often a negative one. The paradigm of the stereotypical Ozarks hillbilly by non-Ozarkers of eras past usually consisted of a poor, uneducated, superstitious people, with the men usually lazy and drunk on moonshine, the "women-folk" doing the majority of the manual labor in addition to raising a shack full of kids… all the inhabitants barefoot and dressed in shabby clothes.

But in recent years, the word "hillbilly", and its associated stereotype, has been misappropriated to an even more hurtful and disparaging category of insult; again, most prominently used by those outside of the Ozarks region. In contemporary times, the word "hillbilly" is sometimes used in place of, or in conjunction with terms like "redneck," "white trash," "trailer trash," and "hick." It is not uncommon to see the contemporary, negative hillbilly stereotypes lumped in with negative stereotypes of Southern culture. Although the Ozarks geographic region is sometimes referred to as the Upland South, and has some cultural similarities, the Ozarks also has many cultural distinctions setting it apart from the Deep South. The goal of this book is to chip away at the negative stereotypes associated with the term "hillbilly" and expose the reality of the actual people of the region. The "real" hillbillies of today, and of yesteryear, are not entirely unlike the people of other rural regions of this Country, of present or the past. What sets them apart would be the environment of the Ozarks and the necessary adaptations made to survive and prosper in this unique geographic region.

The Ozarker, or Ozarks Hillbilly, if you will, has a strong sense of place. This sense of place is a characteristic that was evident with the early pioneers of the region, but also holds true today. Many of the Ozarks' early settlers emigrated from the Appalachian states in the early to mid-1800s. They found a landscape similar to their prior home and had the skills and fortitude to survive in this beautiful, but rugged area. Many early residents came for the inexpensive land; lands that were overlooked by other settlers because of the lack of suitable farming grounds in these rocky hills. Others preferred the inherent seclusion and solitude provided by the remoteness of the Ozarks' steep hills and deep hollows. Theirs is a true love affair with the Ozarks; the sense of place and even pride in these hills can lead to the embracement of the term "hillbilly" as a self-designation for hill folk.

Be it ever-increasing urbanization, growing population, ever-shrinking availability of lands in the Ozarks, or just the mysterious, seductiveness of the region, there is a phenomenon that has been occurring over the last few decades with new immigrants from other regions of the United States. This new phenomenon is called "last one in lock the door." My Ozarks Geography professor in college, Dr. Milt Rafferty, brought this phrase to my attention during his course. As a young person, I had witnessed this several times in several different ways, but Dr. Rafferty actually put it into words. The idea is that generally, retirees from urban areas, or even young professionals, resettle in the Ozarks from cities and states outside the Ozarks, and once they are here, have great disdain for anyone else with a similar plan.

The Ozarks and its sense of place are infectious. It is not difficult to imagine how the newcomers' "last one in lock the door" attitude only amplifies this sense of place for Ozarkers whose families have been in the region for generations. It would be difficult to count how many times, even being an Ozarker myself, that I've been asked two questions: Where are you from? And if the answer is "the Ozarks," then, question number two — how many generations has your family been here? It's as though their measure of your Ozarkerness is based solely on how far back you can trace your family roots in these hills. You can imagine my relief when I found out, after months of genealogical research, that I could trace my own Ozarks lineage back to 1798, with the arrival of my fifth great-grandfather, John McNail, to Potosi (Mine à Breton), Missouri Territory.

There was also another phenomenon that occurred in the Ozarks in the 1970s. The back-to-the-land movement brought many people and their families from urban areas across the country to live in the Ozarks in a simple and sometimes communal lifestyle. These were intentional hillbillies, trying to survive off the land, often in a very primitive way. All three of these groups: multi-generational Ozarkers, new-comers, and back-to-the-landers, all probably have some sense of pride at some level, in holding the designation of "hillbilly."

The Ozarks hillbilly image that we commonly think of today was often created by outsiders (those not from or residing in the Ozarks), and most of the time, this was not a very complimentary image. One of the early examples of this negative image of the Ozarks resident, later to be known as the Ozarks hillbilly, was by Henry Rowe Schoolcraft. Schoolcraft was from a prominent family in New York. In November of 1818, he and another New Yorker, Levi Pettibone, set out into the wilderness of the Ozarks on a three-month, 900-mile journey in search of a rumored lead deposit in the White River Valley. Schoolcraft and Pettibone, both inexperienced, poorly prepared, and unfamiliar with the Ozarks region, spent a great deal of the trek lost and near starvation. There were very few settlers in the region and those they did encounter were most likely responsible for saving the lives of Schoolcraft and Pettibone.

Schoolcraft kept a detailed journal of the flora, fauna, geology and inhabitants of the Ozarks and his published works have been the basis for historical studies of the Ozarks for decades. Unfortunately, even though the settlers were extremely helpful to Schoolcraft, his descriptions of them in his published journals established a negative stereotype of the inhabitants of the Ozarks as a rustic and uneducated people that has endured, to a degree, for 200 years. During the twentieth century, Hollywood movies, comic strips, musicals, and television programs continued to perpetuate the more negative stereotypes of the hillbilly, with additional disparaging attributes added through the years.

To quote the American musician, Beck: "You can't write if you can't relate." I would consider myself an "Ozarks Hillbilly." I've been called a hillbilly as both a compliment and as a hurtful insult. I've heard both on numerous occasions throughout the nearly five decades of my life. My observations of this hillbilly phenomenon are not based on a great deal of academic-style study, although I've spent the better part of my life researching the Ozarks as a passionate hobby. I'm a self-diagnosed romantic-nostalgic when it comes to my interest in the study of the Ozarks. I blame my Ozarks-romantic-nostalgic condition in large part on the marketing of this "Ozarks Hillbilly Image" that was so deeply imprinted on my soul as a child.

Like most children, I had some favorite amusement destinations, and I'm forever grateful for the close proximity of these destinations to our home and that my family had the means to visit them. My favorite amusement destinations did not include Disneyland, Six Flags, or other similar venues, but rather Silver Dollar City, Shepherd of the Hills Farm, and Dogpatch USA. All three of these locations had some association with a hillbilly image, but each in their own way. All three were very impactful on my own paradigm of what a hillbilly was or is, and being an Ozarker myself, where I might "fit in" to the hillbilly designation. To me, all three theme parks had a positive approach to the presentation of the Ozarks hillbilly. Regarding the third, Dogpatch USA, many may find my choice as a positive hillbilly presentation debatable, but I will explain in a moment.

Silver Dollar City, especially in the 1970s and 1980s (and most likely before, but that was before my time), had done a painstakingly good job of theming every aspect of the park to simulate an 1880s Ozarks community. Everything from the amusement rides to the food concessions were presented as accurately as possible in the 1880s Ozarks theme. Pioneer buildings were constructed with hand-hewn logs, (with men, in costume, using a broad axe to construct the buildings). The town square had a rustic general store with jars of preserves, beef jerky, cheeses, and even tobacco and corn cob pipes. During that early era, there were countless craftspeople creating amazing items with traditional skills (basket weaving, cornhusk dolls, blacksmithing, glassblowing, chair caning, candle making, just to name a few).

The amusement rides all had an Ozarks theme as well, sometimes fictitious, but having some element of historical fact. One thing that I will forever remember is the smells: the sulfur smell of the coal smoke from the blacksmith shop, the hickory smoke from the barbeque pits, the sweet aromas of peanut brittle being made at the candy shop and the smell of fresh bread and cookies coming out of the oven at the old mill. The most influential aspect, to me, may have been the people… they were dressed as hillbillies. Of course, there were a few comedic characters, barefoot, in torn-up overalls and slouchy, misshapen hats, but the majority were in calico dresses, or overalls and boots, representing either the rural elite, or the rural poor of the Ozarks… the townsfolk, and the country folk.

I quickly grew to love this place and its inhabitants. This was the Ozarks I wanted to be a part of. Silver Dollar City, in part, made me the Ozarks-nostalgic I am today. Like the term "hillbilly", Silver Dollar City is much different than it was forty years ago. As an amateur historian, I understand the importance of historical context, even in regards to the study of recent history. As a society, we try to improve upon what we've learned in the scientific and social realms. Related to this concept, for me, are a couple childhood memories from Silver Dollar City in the early 1980s. The Silver Dollar City of that time is quite different than it currently is and most likely will not revert back, and yes, maybe in at least some ways, this is for the better.

One thing I do miss is the wagons being pulled around the park by livestock. It was always fascinating to see the horses and mules on the grounds of the theme park. Their presence added to the authenticity of the experience and it was educational for sure. But I can understand the safety concerns as the park grew in popularity. Tens of thousands of guests and mule-drawn wagons don't mix well. Another personal Silver Dollar City story of mine that will most likely never recur (and may not have been repeated in the past forty years), is as follows.

There was one wagon driver that appeared to me, through the analytical eye of my eight-year-old self, to be the real deal hillbilly, not just an employee dressed as one. He was sitting up in the spring seat rather stoically, his worn-out leather boots resting on the toe board so that I could see the holes worn through the bottom of the soles. He had the classic hillbilly beard, long, scraggly and sandy, just like on the Seaton family hillbilly postcards in the gift shops around town. His hat was worn out and pulled kind of low… but it was a real hat, worn out from age and use, not like those worn by the street performers. He didn't smile, and wasn't overly friendly like the other characters in the park. I was sure he drove that wagon and team to work that day from somewhere in the surrounding hills. His well-trained mule team stood there patiently, as though they knew their job was ninety percent photo-op for the passing tourists.

While I was standing there, admiring this perfect example of what I thought was a hillbilly, he took a small, shiny round can out of the front pocket of his faded denim shirt. He opened the can and took out a little pinch of a dark material from inside the can and stuck the material into his bushy beard, about where I thought his mouth should be. After a couple silent moments, he spit out a bit of that stuff, which explained the stain on his beard. I hadn't said one word to the stoic old hillbilly until just then. "Hey, can I try some of that?"

Without a word, the old feller reached back into his shirt pocket and leaned forward just enough to hand me down the little, round, shiny can. I very carefully opened the can and took my own pinch… then I stuck the strange material into my mouth. Immediately my mouth began to burn and my eyes welled up with tears of shock and terror. It tasted horrible and burned my tongue… I spit that stuff out way faster than I ever put it in. The old hillbilly's beard changed shape and I'm pretty sure there was a big grin under there somewhere. "Yuh won't want none of that no more will ya?" Looking back, I don't have any less admiration for that old wagon driver than I did when I first saw him. And I sure don't fault him for his actions. That was his way of teaching me a lesson about a bad habit. For him, it was the right thing to do, and he most likely had good intentions. But that sure wouldn't happen in this day and age.

Shepherd of the Hills Farm was another favorite amusement location of my childhood and continues to be today. The Shepherd of the Hills Farm and outdoor theater are based on The *Shepherd of the Hills* novel by Harold Bell Wright. The 1907 book was written, at least in part, on the location of the park and was a fictional story based on that very location and the surrounding hills and valleys, as well as actual people, or attributes of actual people, in the surrounding community.

Shepherd of the Hills felt like another home for me, much like Silver Dollar City, but in a bit of a different way. Even at an early age, I realized that the "theme park" at Shepherd and the play itself, were based on at least some tangible reality about that portion of the Ozarks that I was not only familiar with, but truly loved. Right there in the park is the iconic "Old Matt's Cabin," the one-time home of John K. and Anna Ross. The Rosses were hosts for Harold Bell Wright when he visited the Ozarks. Similar to Silver Dollar City, the owners and staff of Shepherd of the Hills in the late 1970s and early 1980s did not miss a detail when keeping the theme authentically Ozarkian… at least turn of the nineteenth-twentieth century authentic.

Every staff member of the park was dressed in the typical hillbilly garb, but their interactions with the public were just a bit different. The daytime staff on the farm almost seemed more about education than the entertainment and amusement presented at Silver Dollar City. Their passion for the real history of Shepherd of the Hills really showed through and that passion for Ozarks history was infectious to my young mind. The Shepherd of the Hills Outdoor drama, which occurs in the evenings on the farm, was, and still is, quite the experience for all of the senses. The horses, the square dancers, the whistle of the old steam engine at the mill, and of course, the terrifying masked, torch-bearing Bald Knobbers, are just part of this amazing Ozarks time machine. The outdoor setting with the night sounds of crickets, tree frogs and whippoorwills makes the viewers feel like they are really there, part of the scene. The actors in the play, some of whom are part of this book (Keith Thurman and the Seaton family) were my childhood heroes.

Twenty years later, when I was fortunate enough to play a Bald Knobber a couple nights a week after my day job, I found a whole new respect for these childhood heroes. There is something about Shepherd of the Hills and the traditional Ozarks culture that gets into these peoples' blood. At varying levels, most of these people consider themselves to be hillbillies and they are proud of it. They are proud of the hard work and determination, as well as the values of the early Ozarks settlers that survived in this rugged but beautiful land. Most of these actors are locals, and for some of them, their Shepherd of the Hills personae are not far removed from their day-to-day life.

The third mentioned amusement destination that had such an influence on my perceptions of the hillbilly stereotype, as well as fortifying my Ozarks-nostalgic condition was Dogpatch USA. That mysterious seductiveness of the Ozarks mentioned previously plays a part in my fond memories of this particular venue as well. Dogpatch USA, which has been defunct and closed for the last twenty-five years, was a theme park based on the Li'l Abner comic strip by Al Capp. The location of the theme park was situated south of Harrison, Arkansas at the northern boundary of the Boston Mountains of the Arkansas Ozarks, just a stone's throw from the beautiful and very popular Buffalo River.

The Boston Mountain region of the Ozarks is arguably one of the most beautiful areas of the Ozarks and has some of the most impressive landforms, with the Boston Mountains towering well above the neighboring White River Hills to the north. It's almost like an amplification of all of the other wonderful natural features found elsewhere in the Ozarks: taller mountains, deeper valleys, and more remoteness. Anyone familiar with Li'l Abner, Daisy Mae Yokum and the other Dogpatch characters from Capp's comic strip realizes that it was based on some pretty extreme hillbilly stereotypes, far enough removed from any reality that there is not even a question in young peoples' minds that this is exaggeration and doesn't represent "real" hillbillies. One might even argue, and have a very successful argument, that Dogpatch USA was a substantial promoter of some of the negative hillbilly stereotypes that exist. But speaking for myself,

Dogpatch USA created some of the best memories of my youth and further reinforced my pride in being somewhat of a hillbilly. I believe the major contributing factor was the location.

The northern Arkansas Ozarks is the geographic epicenter of my personal love for the Ozarks region at that age. The Boston Mountains are impressive in size; the surrounding area seemed remote and un-tainted by development at that time. The Buffalo River is in close proximity. This sense of place, the love of the land, the natural features were the foundation for my belief. Secondly, the Dogpatch characters, roaming the park in full costume; the beautiful, yet scantily clad Daisy Mae; the big and powerful, yet dumb Li'l Abner; and the spunky and peculiar Mammy Yokum…these were just local kids dressed up and having fun! The characters and visitors all understood it was fun and that it was an exaggeration, a joke. But it fit.

In contrast, I remember how it made me feel just a little uncomfortable seeing the "token" hillbilly comedians on the Branson music show billboards lining the thirty-five mile stretch of Highway 65 between Springfield and Branson, Missouri. Those characters too are exaggerations, but the images seem to carry even more of a slur. The slight hat-tip to the hillbilly stereotype is overpowered by things that seem disassociated with hill culture. Neon colors, sequined outfits and faces distorted by the omission of dentures not only takes the negative stereotypes to another level, but seems overused and disingenuous.

The third contributing factor to the positive influence on me and my wonderful memories of Dogpatch USA is the attitude of the visitors themselves. I was visiting Dogpatch mainly in my teenage years. My perception was that the attributes of close proximity and affordable entry fees that made a trip to Dogpatch feasible for me were similar for many others. It seemed like a destination for locals, for the most part. It was a day trip destination and it was also, for a theme park anyway, kind of in the middle of nowhere. The closest major town was Harrison, Arkansas. Dogpatch was well off the beaten path and deep in the Ozarks. It was also cheap to get in, a fraction of the cost of Silver Dollar City, but honestly, not the caliber of amusements and attractions as Silver Dollar City either. But that's what made it special.

The visitors, a majority it seemed, were contemporary hill folks, some who probably considered themselves hillbillies. Of course, many were from larger towns like Harrison, Fayetteville or Springfield, but there's no doubt that a lot of the visitors were Ozarkers. The vibe was different than the other, more substantial theme parks with multi-million dollar rides and high-end shows. It was a place where exploration of the Ozarkian and hillbilly kitsch, the Dogpatch cabins, interacting with the comic characters and old-school, carnival type amusements, where imaginative fun and finding new friends made up for what Dogpatch lacked in comparison to the more expensive theme parks in the region. It is difficult to describe, but it was like a bunch of real hillbilly kids, living and playing within their own cartoon. We could make fun of ourselves, but also be proud of an exaggeration of our culture. It was like a massive playground, custom made for us.

As I mentioned in the previous three examples, the commercialization of the hillbilly image can be positive in nature, light-hearted and fun. But I do have another personal experience where the exploitation of the hillbilly image and hill culture took a dark turn, creating feelings of sorrow and pity. This particular story is what ignited the idea for this collaborative book effort about hillbillies between Tom Koob and myself. This story also did not occur in the Ozarks, but rather the Appalachian Mountains of northeastern Georgia.

In addition to numerous hobbies including reading Ozarks fiction and non-fiction, creating art, and spending as much time in the Ozarks outdoors as possible, I am also a movie buff. One film that has always fascinated me is the movie *Deliverance*. This 1972 film was produced and directed by John Boorman and starred Burt Reynolds, as well as James Dickey, who was the author of the 1970 novel of the same name on which the screenplay was based. *Deliverance*, nearly fifty years after its release, is still a cult classic. When the film opened in 1972, it pushed boundaries with adult language and violence, which is not necessarily uncommon, but there were other themes introduced by the film that were more shocking and disturbing to many.

I remember my mother telling me that she was about six months pregnant with me when she and my father went to the theater to see the film. My Dad was, at the time, and still is, an avid outdoorsman, and enjoys hunting and fishing, and I believe those elements of the *Deliverance* movie is what appealed to him and encouraged him to purchase a pair of tickets for himself and Mom. Years later, my mother told me that she became physically ill watching the movie and had to leave before the show was over. She said it was probably due more to the disturbing scenes in the movie than it was the effects of her pregnancy. The other thing I remember both of my parents mentioning about the movie was how it gave a very derogatory portrayal of Appalachian mountain people, or Appalachian hillbillies, if you will. They never elaborated on what the elements of this negative portrayal were.

As a teenager, I finally saw the film on cable television in the late 1980s. Things I would hear as a kid on float trips on the Buffalo, and other Ozarks rivers, like "paddle faster, I hear banjos," and "squeal like a pig," followed by boisterous laughter, finally made some sense. It also brought back what my parents had said about the portrayal of the mountain people, but I was either too young or inexperienced at that time to fully understand the depth of their concern about that issue. The movie's canoeing, camping, hunting and fishing, and the lush green mountains of northeastern Georgia had a familiarity to me, like the Ozarks region where I had been raised. I was hooked on the movie and watched it numerous times over the years. I had always wanted to see the Chattooga River where the movie was filmed and even float that challenging waterway if possible.

Years later, when I was in my mid-thirties, I had a trade conference to attend in North Carolina. I was in charge of transporting a trailer full of booth and display items from Missouri, cross-country to North Carolina. This was my opportunity to see the Chattooga River and the *Deliverance* country of Rabun County, Georgia. I was looking forward to a road trip through Appalachia and the Great Smoky Mountains, then on into northeastern Georgia and northwestern South Carolina in search of wonderful scenery and the actual filming locations of the movie.

During my Internet research and trip planning in the days leading up to the trek, I stumbled across what would be a unique opportunity in an obscure advertisement. The ad stated that you could receive an autographed photo of "Banjo Boy" Billy Redden from the movie *Deliverance*.

Banjo Boy, played by the then, sixteen-year-old Billy Redden, is an iconic figure in the movie. Banjo Boy was the character who had the musical standoff with actor Ronny Cox, who played the character of Drew Ballinger. In this scene, Banjo Boy was seated on a porch swing of an old cabin with a banjo in hand and "Drew" had a guitar that he brought along for that fateful canoe trip. The two musicians proceeded to spar back and forth, mocking each other's rapidly picked notes until they broke into a melodious mountain tune that would not only become the most memorable score in the movie (topping the radio charts in 1973), but also became iconic as the theme song for the stereotyped hillbilly image. What left just as much of an impression on movie-goers as the catchy "Dueling Banjos" tune, was the physical appearance of Banjo Boy. His skinny frame was clothed in a drab, brown and worn-out shirt. His mannerisms and expressions were quirky and odd. And his facial features were unique, with thin lips and squinty eyes. Actor Ned Beatty, whose character "Bobby Trippe," made a statement in the movie which explained what image the director was trying to portray when he said "Talk about genetic deficiencies. Isn't that pitiful?"

What caught my eye and really got my trip-planning wheels turning was that the Internet ad also stated that you could actually meet "Banjo Boy" Billy Redden in Clayton, Georgia and have him autograph the photo in person! I figured this was a unique opportunity to meet the actual person that was an icon of such a cult-classic movie, as well as the source of so many float and camping trip puns, phrases and wise-cracks that I had heard most of my life. So, I scribbled down the phone number listed in the advertisement and made sure that my route to the Carolinas took me through Clayton, Georgia.

A day before I arrived in Clayton, Georgia, I called the phone number I had scribbled down from the Internet advertisement. Almost immediately, I knew the pending meeting with "Banjo

Boy" Billy Redden would be an interesting one. It sounded like the gentleman on the other end of the phone call was not only the "businessman" of the autographed photo endeavor, but quite possibly, Billy's caretaker as well. He said that although Billy lived there at his place, a more appropriate meeting would be over breakfast the following day. He also asked if I would pick up Billy from his third-shift as a stocker at the local Wal-Mart at 7:30 in the morning and take him to breakfast. I agreed to these terms immediately and without much thought. Very quickly, my mind was attempting to process the situation which began to tear away at all my preconceived notions. Why would someone as well-known and famous as the Banjo Boy from *Deliverance* be working third shift as a stocker? Why was this other individual setting up autograph signing appointments with a total stranger for such a celebrity? Why was I trusted with the task of picking up said celebrity and taking him to breakfast, not to mention getting him home safe and sound?

The next morning I was right on time. It wasn't hard to find the Wal-Mart in Clayton. It was a beautiful, sunny morning and the sunlight was lighting up the lush green hills in the mountain town. As instructed, I pulled up to the back of the store and parked my vehicle. It wasn't long before a couple emerged from the steel door of the employee entrance at the back of the building. One of the couple was a young woman, probably in her early thirties, wearing a blue Wal-Mart smock and a friendly smile. She was escorting an older man, diminutive in stature and also wearing a smock.

"Are you Curtis?" the friendly and smiling woman asked with a sweet Georgia accent.

"Yes, ma'am, I am. I'm here to pick up Billy and take him to breakfast and visit a bit," I replied, still feeling awkward in the surreal situation.

"Well, thank you sir. Ya know, we just like to check folks out and make sure they are nice people before we send Billy here off with 'em. Thank you so much for giving him a ride."

So Billy climbed into my vehicle and we made our way to a nearby cafe for breakfast. He was quiet and soft-spoken, sometimes difficult to understand. I do believe that he stated that he actually owned the cafe at one time. Billy was greeted heartily at the diner. They already knew that he would be having grits for breakfast. It was very clear that the whole town knew Billy. And it had become increasingly clear that they all "took care of" Billy as well. Although everyone was friendly, I got the feeling that everyone was making sure that I was of a good character to be spending time with their Billy. As mentioned previously, Billy was quiet and didn't say much unless asked questions… not much of a conversationalist. The one exception was the subject of grits. The man repeated several times how much he loved grits.

After breakfast, I asked if he would mind going for a drive and show me some of the filming locations from the movie before going home. He agreed and it was so exciting to see some of the sites from the movie. It was a relief that even after forty years, not much had changed at all. Some of the roads had been paved and some of the buildings were more decrepit. The beautiful Chattooga River still ran wild and free. I wasn't able to glean a lot of information from Billy, but I did learn that he was a river guide for some time, telling tourists about the filming locations on the river.

He was also proud of having the opportunity to have cameo scenes in a couple other movies over the years (again, typecast in his role as Banjo Boy). He said that most of the actors on the set of *Deliverance* were kind to him. He was sixteen at the time. The director and crew came to his school and visited his classroom. He was chosen out of all his classmates. He didn't know how to play banjo (and still doesn't); so the *Deliverance* crew picked another boy out of his class that did know how to play the banjo. In the famous scene, although Billy is strumming the banjo, the production crew had altered Billy's shirt so that the other boy, hidden behind Billy, could run his arm through the sleeve and work the fretting on the neck of the banjo. Surely after forty years, Billy understood that he was cast for his "unique" physical features, but I sure wasn't going to ask him that question.

When I dropped Billy off at his home, it felt almost awkward getting the autographed photo from him. At that time, the whole situation still felt quite unreal, but there were other emotions taking effect. The gravity of my parents' comments about the very negative portrayal of mountain people in the film finally broke through the levity of the wisecracks and float-trip jokes that I had accepted for years. Billy and others that had been cast in his community were exploited... hillbilly-exploitation, if you will. I suddenly had a new awareness when standing face to face with the person, Billy Redden, not the character, Banjo Boy. At that moment, I felt a sense of guilt for wanting his autograph, for my intention to acquire a real and tangible souvenir of an icon of hillbilly mythology. But was I also exploiting this man? Whether it was for the sake of literature, art, other creative expression or financial gain, many have perpetuated negative stereotypes of the hillbilly. The movie *Deliverance* changed Billy Redden to "Banjo Boy" forever. My only hope is that Billy has a peace and comfort with it.

As mentioned previously, the goal of this book is to strip away the layers of negative stereotypes that are associated with the word "hillbilly," whether those stereotypes were created intentionally or organically through various perceptions over the decades and to find what it means to be a real hillbilly and the positive attributes of that type of persona. It appears that outside of the Ozarks region itself, the term "hillbilly" is commonly used in a negative connotation. It is very interesting, the power of words and their ability to morph in meaning and context over time, influenced by history, art, literature, and media. There are also the influences of basic human nature. One may refer to someone as a hillbilly to express their own superiority over another because of social, economic, or class factors. On the other hand, one may proclaim themselves a hillbilly for that basic tribal urge to be associated with a group that is so closely linked with their beloved Ozarks.

As surely as time changes, so does the Ozarks, not only the landscape itself, due to progress and population, but the culture. I feel that many of the qualities associated with the traditional positive stereotypes of the hillbilly are fading away into history; self-sufficient survivors, rugged individualists, rural and tough, and of the land. Modern technology, paved roads and improved transportation and improved, global communications to even the most remote areas of the Ozarks have had the inevitable effect of diluting character attributes that would define what we would consider the traditional hillbilly. Just in the last twenty-five years, I've seen significant change in what I would consider to be Ozarks culture.

Harold Bell Wright, famous writer and author of one of the best-selling novels of all time, *The Shepherd of the Hills*; Vance Randolph, thought by many to be the greatest Ozarks folklorist/ collector to date; and Otto Rayburn, Ozarks boosterism writer and Ozarks magazine publisher, all had a couple things in common. All three promoted a nostalgic and for the most part, positive image of the Ozarks hillbilly, and what they felt were the attributes that made the Ozarks hillbilly exceptional. Secondly, through the stroke of their pens or keys of their typewriters, they expressed their lamentation for the fading of what they considered the traditional Ozarks hill person or hillbilly and the dilution of traditional Ozarks culture (which for them, for the most part, would be the seventy-five-year period between the Civil War and World War II). Their passion for the nostalgic Ozarks was embraced by many and criticized heavily by those that wanted to see the primitive Ozarks progress with the rest of the Country. For Wright, it was witnessing the coming of the railroad to the heart of the Taney County Ozarks about 1905 that would have the potential of bringing thousands of visitors previously prohibited by primitive roads. For Randolph, it was the new systems of paved roads and highways that catered to the ever increasingly popular automobile that would bring outside influences that would dilute the dialects and cultures kept primitive by the remoteness of the rugged Ozarks hills. For Rayburn, (who must have been the most conflicted of them all because his way of making a living was promoting the Ozarks), it was the ever growing tourist industry and influx of retirees to the Ozarks from urban areas from all over the Nation.

Like Wright, Randolph, and Rayburn, I probably fall within the romantic/nostalgic category myself, in regards to my interests in the Ozarks region and hillbilly culture. The sentimentalism of this character trait can be emotionally cumbersome sometimes, especially in regards to the inevitable progress and change destined for the beautiful Ozarks that I love. In my brief forty-eight years on this Earth, in and of the Ozarks, I have personally witnessed ever-increasing change, population growth and urbanization of the Ozarks hills. I can say that I've also witnessed the "dilution" of the "traditional" Ozarks culture that Randolph and Rayburn foretold decades before. Of course, there are personal perceptions of what I would consider "traditional" Ozarks culture and hillbilly traits, but even on this personal level, I have seen those fade and change as well.

When I'm on the Buffalo River trail in the springtime, especially on a warm, sunny day, I will find myself taking a break on one of the many rocky, vista-view bluff tops overlooking the magnificent Buffalo River below. The many canoes and kayaks floating down the river below form a seemingly endless and colorful chain that extends the run of the river as far as one can see both upstream and downstream. The beautiful Buffalo River has increased exponentially in popularity over the past twenty-five years, and rightly so. Its beauty is like no other and thank goodness it was preserved from being dammed nearly fifty years ago. The tremendous growth in the river's visitation could be because of the explosive urban growth of the nearby metropolitan areas of Northwest Arkansas or the similar population growth in the Springfield-Branson area of Missouri to the north. Or it could be because it is simply being discovered by many more due to advancements in communication, like the Internet or social media.

As I hear the murmur of laughter and chatter from the colorful serpentine chain of kayaks and canoes on the river hundreds of feet below my bluff top perch, I wonder if, for the river floaters this is their Ozarks cultural experience; if there are primitive elements to their Buffalo River float trip and the compelling pristineness of the surrounding Ozarks hills that makes them feel at least a little bit hillbilly for the day. Things have changed on the river. Not just its popularity, but the availability of wider highways and larger, more modern and sleek outfitter stores and rental facilities. I know that just twenty-five years ago, I felt like a "hillbilly for the day," when my Buffalo River experiences contained what I felt were real characteristics of hillbilly culture. For my friends and me, our float trip included the

Ozarkian experience of just getting to the river itself. The first stop would be to acquire sustenance for the float. Would we stop at Coursey's Smoked Meats in St. Joe, Arkansas? It was, and still is, family run, a real-life smokehouse business started back in 1945. The original log smokehouse still stands to this day. The friendly folks there would build us the most delicious "taste-of-the-Ozarks" smoked ham and smoked cheese sandwiches and wrap them up in foil for us to take to the river. The next stop would be the canoe outfitter. This establishment was basically a shack along the highway with several canoes of various colors, ages, materials, and various states of damage, positioned around a parking area of weeds and gravel. But we weren't there for just canoes; this particular outfitter would also sell limited cases of "bootleg" beer... for this was, and still is, a dry County. With our bootleg beer, smoked sandwiches, beat-up canoes and an afternoon on what is one of the most beautiful rivers in the Ozarks, we truly felt like we were experiencing the best of hillbilly livin'!

Time, communication technology, transportation improvements, education improvements, population growth and in-migration. All of these factors and more influence not only Ozarks culture from a regional standpoint, but the hillbilly image as well. What, if any, "traditional" Ozarks characteristic or positive hillbilly trait will remain? And what are those "positive" or "traditional" or truly "Ozarks Hillbilly" traits? Hopefully, this book will bring forth some of those answers.

Curtis Copeland

# Chapter 1

## Hillcrofters and Hillbillies

*The Ozarks* has received plenty of attention for its scenery, its people and its culture. It has been viewed with admiration, disdain and apathy. Some of what has been written about these ancient mountains and the folks they shelter has been praiseworthy; some not so much.

To understand the Ozarks way of life requires more than a visit, more than an assessment of demographics, more than a casual reading of Ozarks literature. These studies can certainly create an impression. But to understand the region's people, it helps to "sit a spell" and talk to them. Listening to their own stories — stories of triumph and tragedy, failure and fulfillment, happiness and heartbreak — imparts a better understanding of the real person. The epithet "hillbilly" probably conjures a negative image to many. But let's take a closer look.

In many ways, the Buffalo River Valley of northern Arkansas can be viewed as a microcosm of the Ozarks at large. A beautiful area, blessed with bubbling springs, clear flowing streams, expansive forests and soaring rock bluffs, the Buffalo Valley resisted human settlement. But people did come.

Around 1835, Abraham Villines brought his family into the upper Buffalo region. He settled in the unspoiled mountain wilderness that resembled his home back in the Tennessee Appalachians. Abraham's grandson William built a log home for his bride Rebecca in 1850 where their son James was born in 1854. James became known as "Beaver Jim" for his trapping skills. Jim married Sarah Arbaugh and built his own homeplace

28

within sight of the Buffalo. The Villines homestead sheltered the family for generations and remains today as a fine example of Ozark architecture.

The Villines flourished in and around Ponca, Arkansas on the upper Buffalo. They farmed and raised stock. They operated a general store and a grist mill in Boxley Valley. They hunted the forests and fished the streams. And they helped sustain a community and culture that retained old Ozarks traditions and resisted outside influence.

But change was inevitable. Better roads and bridges eventually made the region more accessible and visitors came for the Ozarks scenery and to float the Buffalo River. The old ways were harder and harder to maintain. Electricity, radio, television and the internet infiltrated deep into the once isolated canyon.

The Buffalo River itself was threatened by plans to dam it. But it was saved and became the first National River. The National Park Service controls a corridor along the entire 150 mile length of the Buffalo now. They have made efforts to preserve the river and the land and the wildlife with reasonable success. Efforts to conserve the Ozarks culture are more challenging. Perhaps the best that can be done is to document what was, photograph what still is and gather the memories. The land and water can be protected, but it is much harder to preserve a way of life.

***Beaver Jim Villines cabin at Ponca***

Wanda Doylene (Villines) Donaldson was born March 1, 1946 in Ponca, Arkansas. She arrived at home with the assistance of her grandma Evans. Wanda was the youngest girl in the family with three brothers and three sisters.

The Villines lived in a quaint home snugged up against the hillside above Ponca. Their home had three main rooms and an upstairs loft. Cooking was done on a wood stove which also provided heat along with a wood-fired pot-bellied stove. There was no running water and no electricity.

Wanda's father Doyle kept some cattle, a dairy cow, chickens and free-range hogs. Doyle grew a corn crop which they would harvest, haul to the mill and have it ground into corn meal. He cut timber for the local sawmill. Wanda's mother Ethel kept house and tended her children. The Villines had a one-acre vegetable garden. They ate well. The Villines also cultivated and sold medicinal plants like ginseng and golden seal. They carefully protected both their home-grown and wild sources of herbs.

Milk, cream and homemade butter were kept in a near-by spring. The spring was also their main source of water. There was a shallow well on the property, but Wanda says the spring water was much colder and sweeter. As a child, Wanda and her siblings made up their own games, playing hopscotch in the dusty yard. Sometimes they played card games.

In the evenings after supper, they would get together with family and friends, singing songs to the accompaniment of guitars and fiddles. Wanda says her entire family was musical and there are many accomplished musicians in her lineage including Merle Haggard. Wanda herself is a talented singer and songwriter having received recognition for her work from the American Song Festival in 1984.

Wanda started her education at Beechwoods, a one-room schoolhouse near Lost Valley. She later attended the small rural elementary school at Compton and graduated from high school at Harrison.

Growing up, Wanda's mother made the family's clothes from hand-me-downs, brightly printed flour sacks, and the occasional store-bought fabrics. Wanda says she got her first pair of shoes at age nine. She distinctly remembers the smell of those shoes — like the mixture of sawdust and kerosene spread on the floor of the general store in Ponca.

Wanda's home was in an idyllic location, surrounded by virgin forest, nestled in verdant Boxley Valley formed by the Buffalo River. She often went to the river — bathing, swimming, fishing, noodling. It was a wild and wonderful place.

Wanda says she doesn't recall seeing any tourists or canoers when she was growing up. But she does remember the uproar caused when the National Park Service began seizing land under eminent domain for the proposed Buffalo National River in the 1960s.

The Corps of Engineers had long wanted to dam the Buffalo and create a reservoir that would permanently flood much of the pristine river valley. Opposition to the dam won out and the free-flowing stream was established as the first National River in 1972. Many residents lost private use of their land to the project, but Wanda admits that the National River was better than a permanent loss to a large reservoir.

Wanda says, "We never knew we were poor. We lived a good life and I didn't realize we were any different than anyone else until I went to high school in Harrison. I never heard the word "hillbilly" growing up. But now I know I am a hillbilly. I'm proud that it means I'm honest, straight-forward and tough. I'm proud of my family and my ancestry."

Wanda Donaldson translated the skills she learned growing up along the Buffalo River into a successful career in real estate. Her knowledge of the hills and her genuineness with people made her a natural fit for helping others make a home in the Ozarks.

Wanda has worked and lived with her husband Jerry in Shell Knob, Missouri for several years. She enjoys visiting Ponca, the Buffalo still flowing clear and cold through the deep green valley. She can visit friends and family and look in on the graves of her Villines and Arbaugh ancestors at Beechwoods Cemetery.[1]

Wanda (Villines) Donaldson's story paints a realistic portrait of the joys and difficulties of mountain life; an honest account of the hillfolk, the mountain people, the hillbillies that carved a respectable life out of a beautiful, but challenging environment. Could the common accepted view of the hillbilly be wrong or misguided? Could these hillfolk have more positive traits than are often portrayed in the stereotypical presentation? Perhaps we should reassess our viewpoint. Maybe there is much more beyond the mass produced image than what we imagine.

*Wanda (Villines) Donaldson's childhood home*

If someone called you a hillbilly, how would you react? Your answer might vary wildly depending on the context, who was applying the moniker, your socio-economic background, and your place of origin. The term has been in use for well over a century, generally carrying a negative connotation; yet at times embraced and seen as a tribute to one's independence, strength of character, and commitment to traditional and natural values.

The term "hillbilly" is most often recognized as having linguistic roots from the Celtic Ulster-Scottish. Scots immigrated to Ulster (today primarily Northern Ireland) in significant numbers from the 1400s to the 1800s. These movements of people were partially the result of normal shifts of populations, but primarily due to political, social and economic forces.

The Celts trudged a long and torturous path from central Europe circa 1200 BC, west into France and Spain, and by the mid-first millennium into the British Isles. As they migrated or were pursued, the Celts carried their rich traditions of language, arts and culture. The Celtic way of life took solid roots and developed into the Gaelic culture in what is today Ireland, Scotland, and portions of England.

Celtic life retained strong beliefs tied to religion, warrior culture and rugged individualism. The Celts' religion was often focused on the natural world, but these beliefs waned as Christianity expanded during the first millennium. The Celts brought iron making to the British Isles and employed practical farming and animal husbandry methods. Their strong family ties led to a clan culture.

Celtic clans held fast to their rugged lands and life in Scotland, Ireland and England. Assailed by the Romans, Norse invaders, tyrannical monarchs and English conquerors, the Celts remained dedicated to their clan and their chief.

Nathaniel Harris describes some of the basis for Gaelic clan culture in *Heritage of Scotland*:

"So in traditional society each clan could be regarded as an extended family whose members looked to the current chief as their 'father', committed to protect them and entitled to call on them to follow him to war. The kinship basis of clan society explains the existence of Highland customs such as the 'open house' hospitality of the chiefs, the preservation of elaborate genealogies, and the intense loyalties and bitter feuds of the clansmen."[2]

Harris goes on to characterize some cultural elements of the clan:

"Similar feelings are evoked by the ceilidh, the night gatherings in a cottage or croft where neighbors met to sing and dance to the fiddle or pipes, to tell stories from the clan's history or expatiate on the doings of brownies, kelpies and other supernatural beings." [3]

Although many cultures have similar traits, it is not difficult to draw a connection between the Scottish relationship to the land, close kinship ties, superstition, and cultural expression to the mores and ways of life of the Ozarks mountain people.

"'Ah!' said a Scotchman who came from Glasgow to examine a mining proposition in the Ozarks. 'This reminds me of my ain Heelands.' He delighted in the rolling ranges of green-clad hills, the precipices and rock-covered slopes along the clear streams he felt much at home." [4]

A self-described "Yankee foreigner", Josh Heston, founder of stateoftheozarks.net, has studied the Ozarks since 1998. With a desire to understand his Welsh heritage more fully, Josh has delved into Ozarks culture and its consistent roots in Celtic traits and lore. Josh says, "The early Scots/Irish were a thinking people with a sophisticated cultural narrative. Their societal structure was based on an honor culture to protect and defend the clan. I think this explains much of what we see in true Ozarkian customs and lifestyles — independence, individuality and above all else, good character."[5]

Celtic/Gaelic clan life was disrupted and altered by several events over the course of history. Integrated into the wider British Isles and ultimately dispersed across the globe, this way of life adapted to new environments while retaining the strengths of its culture.

During the Plantation of Ulster, starting in the early 17th century, Irish land was confiscated by the English and Lowland Scots were enticed to relocate to sections of northern Ireland. The purposes of the Plantation were to subjugate and punish the Irish who had rebelled against England, populate the undeveloped region of northern Ireland, strengthen Protestantism in Ulster, and exert more control over the Gaelic region.

Throughout much of the 17th century, the Stuarts, with strong Scottish ties, ruled the British Isles. Eventually deposed, James Francis Edward Stuart and his son Charles Edward Stuart, "Bonnie Prince Charlie", led the Jacobite (from *Jacobus*, the Latin version of *James*) uprisings of the 18th century in an attempt to retake the British throne and establish a Catholic monarchy. The Jacobites were unsuccessful and their cause exacerbated tensions between the Scottish and British, Protestants and Catholics, and the clans and the monarchy.[6]

Between 1717 and 1775, nearly a quarter million Scots-Irish people emigrated from Ulster to the American colonies. These were primarily Protestant tenant farmers who had led successful lives raising flax for linen and sheep for wool. They were so successful at their trades that England enacted the Woolens Act in 1699 which limited exporting of wool and cloth by northern

Ireland only to England.

In the early 1700s, rack-renting was instituted which allowed the wealthy landowners to raise the rent on leased land. This practice began forcing the Ulster farmers off their property. Then came the drought years of 1714 to 1719. Flax crops failed and wool production fell. Driven off their land, squeezed economically and battered by collapsing markets, many Ulster families fled to America.[7]

The Highland Clearances occurred from the mid-eighteenth to the mid-nineteenth century. The Clearances were driven by many factors: social, political and economic. Ongoing tensions between the northern Highlanders of Scotland and the English were brought to a head by the Jacobite revolt. The unsuccessful uprising resulted in the forced eviction of many highland clan members. The Highlanders were banned from carrying arms and wearing tartans or kilts. The period revamped traditional agricultural methods in the Scottish Highlands and Islands, damaged the clan system and forced many Scots off their land.

One purpose of the Clearances was to adapt land uses in the relatively poor highland soil. The Scots had managed their land individually and in groups or clans for centuries. The Clearances provided a system that forcibly moved some of the Highlanders off the land and compelled others to work as tenants in communal agricultural and fishing industries. The raising of sheep was expanded significantly in the region. The individual communal land holdings were called crofts.

Following the Clearances, the crofts were often not successful in adequately supporting their tenants and many crofters emigrated from the Scottish Highlands and Islands to escape a subsistence way of life. Despite the association with the Clearances, crofts and crofters carry a generally positive or at least neutral connotation. Crofts still exist today. The term "hillcrofter" has been used to describe the Scottish Highlanders who live and work on these small communal farms and in more recent times has been applied to caretakers of the Ozarks environment and culture.

Scots have a well-deserved reputation as an emigration prone people. They have successfully settled in areas throughout the world, particularly in regions once part of the British Empire. Large numbers of Irish and Scottish immigrated to America from the 1700s into the 1900s. Events like the Plantation of Ulster and the Highland Clearances were part of the cause for these movements of people. But clearly, much of this emigration can be traced to poverty and famine, particularly, the Potato Famines of the 1800s. The Great Famine in Ireland from 1845 to 1849 resulted from a potato blight which destroyed the potato crop, a staple food of much of Ireland. The catastrophe resulted in about one million deaths and another million escaped through emigration.

The Highland Potato Famine lasted about ten years, starting in 1846. Although longer in duration, the blight in Scotland resulted in fewer deaths than the Irish counterpart. But this event did continue the trend of damage to the clan system and resulted in significant emigration from Scotland, including to the United States.

Many of the Scots and Irish who came to America in the 18th and 19th centuries settled in the Appalachia and Ohio valley regions. Perhaps they were dissuaded from populating the more traditional English regions of New England. Or perhaps they were attracted by the similarities of these mountainous areas to their homelands in Scotland and Ireland. But come they did in significant numbers. Many of these Celtic people eventually made their way to the Ozarks region.

Early Ozarks settlers were clearly not all of Scotch or Irish descent. Immigrants to America came from many regions and some from England, France, Germany and other European countries eventually settled in the Ozarks. Some of these nationalities established prosperous communities, particularly along the riverine fringes of the Ozarks highlands. Germans founded towns along the Missouri River like Westphalia and Hermann that retain distinct Germanic traditions and culture. Freistatt in Lawrence County, Missouri is situated in the upland prairie, but more interior section of the Ozarks. Freistatt retains very strong ties to its German roots. Small enclaves were established by Poles at Pulaskifield in Missouri and Italians at Tontitown, Arkansas. In the eastern Ozarks, the French founded trading posts and communities along the Mississippi river that still carry their influence.

The number of Black Americans in the Ozarks mountainous interior was never very large. Prior to the Civil War, there were slave owners, but most of these were along the perimeter rivers of the Ozarks region. The postbellum Ozarks gradually saw a diminution of Blacks. Many freed Blacks left the area for work in the more industrial regions. Violent racism reduced the number of African Americans even more, particularly in the first decades of the 20th century. Blacks were driven out of many of the towns and cities of the Ozarks and small communities founded by Blacks were eventually depopulated. "Sundown towns" throughout the region explicitly forbid black residents.[8]

The variety of nationalities and ethnic groups in the Ozarks certainly adhered to the melting pot nature of the United States to some degree. But the upland Ozarks seems to have carried particularly strong ties to the Celtic culture.

Celtic peoples who immigrated to the United States shared many customs and folkways. But they did not always share religion. The Jacobites were staunch Catholics or Anglicans. Williamites were equally fervent Protestants. The Scots-Irish who settled in Appalachia and eventually the Ozarks, were almost exclusively Protestant. One exception is the Irish conclave that temporarily established a Catholic community on the Eleven Point River prior to the Civil War. In the hill country, small Protestant congregations were ubiquitous and played a significant role in the development of cultural and moral beliefs in the Ozarks.

The small churches were dominated by Baptist and Methodist denominations, but there were and are various sects and splinter groups of Protestantism throughout the Ozarks mountain area. Baptists were successful here in part due to their non-hierocratic organization and the independence of each congregation. Methodism's use of itinerant and lay preachers, its concentration on the "common" man, and promotion through camp meetings appealed to the hillfolk.[9]

Some of the images of the hillbilly have become associated with religious beliefs and practices, particularly those of the more fundamentalist sects. On one extreme, the hillbilly is sometimes portrayed as a strict, religious moralist steeped in a life of piety. Other images present a stereotype who takes part in extraordinary religious practices like speaking in tongues, faith healing and the handling of snakes. In the most negative portrait, the hillbilly is presented as completely non-religious, living a life devoid of moral guidance, even to the point of perverse sexuality and little concern for human life. As with most "hillbilly" portraits, these assignations are exaggerated and do not represent the mountain people as a whole.

Religion has played only one part in the development of the stereotypical hillbilly image. Class and economic distinctions, regional biases, political expediency, entertainment, and tourism promotion have all played a role in perpetuating the hillbilly perception. So how did the hillbilly become so attached to the Ozarks?

Americans of Celtic ancestry were often at the vanguard of the country's western movement. They moved into and settled the Appalachia region and later the Ozarks. These areas seem to hold some mystique that appealed to their nature. Perhaps, it was merely the rough, hilly landscape that had nurtured their ancestors for so long. Or perhaps, it was the insular qualities of the hills that allowed them to hold on to their culture, avoid authoritarian influences, and remain independent.

Held close by their environment, their families and their culture, these mountain people retained traits of their ancestry that would resist outside influence and they were steeped in their own world view. There were certainly contact with and influence from people of other cultures and to some degree the outside world. But the Ozarks mountain people largely held to the old ways throughout the nineteenth century and well into the twentieth century.

The hillfolks did what they did to survive. Existence required adapting to their environment and living off the land. Shelters were created from local materials, usually wood and stone. The traditional log cabin is ubiquitous throughout the Ozarks region and although these homes certainly varied in size and workmanship, there are some that have lasted well over one hundred years. Examples of finely fitted dove-tail joints in the walls, smooth puncheon floors and dry-laid stone fireplaces attest to the craftsmanship and toil of these pioneers.

*Aunt Cassie Wheeler*

Sustenance was provided through multiple sources. Water is abundant throughout most of the Ozarks. Living near a consistent spring was desirable as a source of fresh water and primitive refrigeration. Hunting, trapping and fishing were the primary sources of food, particularly in the early days. As more people moved into the region, subsistence farming became integrated into the mountain existence. The raising of livestock was generally on a small scale, but the family who could butcher and preserve a hog periodically improved their lot significantly. Foraging and the collecting of wild plants improved the nutrition and meal variety for a hill family.

Home life was coordinated by the women. The toil of everyday chores was never ending. Skills in food preparation, clothes making, cleaning, child rearing, and home remedies were essential to an isolated mountain existence. Women's work was never done; but they persisted, often pregnant and raising numerous children.

Social life for these "hillbillies" was limited. In the early days, schools and churches were widely scattered, if available at all. If there was entertainment, it occurred within the family group or with a few neighbors. Some form of musical entertainment was always important to the mountain culture. If restricted by religious or moral code, people simply sang. They sang the old songs carried down by generations — songs of long forgotten kings or queens, songs of jilted lovers, sad songs of lost children.

Some musical instruments were brought by these settlers when they moved into the Ozarks. Smaller, often stringed instruments like the fiddle, banjo or the mountain dulcimer, were common and valued. Some hillfolk made their own instruments, sometimes stringed, but often percussive like the jawbone, bones or washboard. If unaccompanied, foot stomping or a brisk jig provided an irresistible cadence.

The hillfolks' music held strains of the Scots-Irish and English melodies. The refrains carried the lilt and drone of the Old World songs. The mountain people adapted this music to their own needs and tastes.

Interaction between the sexes offered some interesting challenges. Restricted by geography and sometimes moral codes, young people had to be creative to find and connect with a potential mate. The play party was often one of the best means for achieving this. A family would sponsor a get together, usually at their home, inviting relatives and neighbors. The young people would gather together in a room and sing together. Sometimes dancing was involved, but often it was not. Simple songs, often with repetitious choruses and sometimes multiple verses, created an atmosphere of fun and potential conversation. It is not too difficult to picture an excited group of young people, the girls wrapped in their frilliest gingham dresses and the boys wearing their cleanest overalls, trying to catch the eye of their amorous intention.

Social interaction also occurred as part of regular work and life. Hog scalds, barn raisings, quilting bees, hunting trips and crop harvesting all contributed to interaction among the mountain folk. They appreciated and relied on these communal efforts.

The language of the hillfolk retained structure, syntax, usage, pronunciation and references to the ancient Celtic voice and Old and Middle English. Supported by isolation and common interest, mountain people spoke a dialect that both identified them as unique and set them apart from the "outside" world.

In his work, *The Ozarks An American Survival of Primitive Society*, Vance Randolph says, "Whatever the eminent scholar may think about it, every layman who travels much in the Ozark country knows that some of the older natives do speak a peculiar jargon derived doubtless from the dialect of the southern Appalachians, containing many words and phrases which are almost unintelligible to ordinary people from other parts of the United States."[10]

Randolph's *Down in the Holler* does an excellent job of connecting the unique dialect of the Ozarks region to the English spoken in Chaucerian and Shakespearian Britain. It is so easy to hear these words spoken by hillfolk and make the presumption that their language is the result of ignorance. But the truth is the Ozarks dialect in its purist usage contains many elements of Middle and Elizabethan English. Ozarkian is not crude; it is based on an older, purer form of our language.

Randolph studied the Ozarks dialect during his long sojourn in the region in the early 20th century. He heard, recorded and documented hundreds of words, phrases, pronunciations and meanings that identify a speech with roots in three hundred year-old English. "The Ozark hillfolk are the descendants of certain adventurous souls who left the Appalachians more than a century ago. They have been, until recently, even more isolated than their Appalachian relatives. It is not surprising, then, that the Ozark speech is full of archaisms."[11]

The hillfolk of the Ozarks may have used the term "hillbilly" to refer to themselves for generations, but it did not show up in media usage until the late nineteenth century. The Cincinnati Enquirer newspaper of October 18, 1881 printed a short item with the headline, "Nicholasville, Kentucky The Town Taken By Roughs". The story reads as follows: "This has been Court-day, and a quiet one, until about dark, when ten or fifteen roughs known locally as 'Hill Billies,' undertook to take the city. They, by firing off pistols, shouting and other boisterous conduct, created great consternation among our citizens, and the police endeavored to arrest them, but without avail, as they were too many for him."

It would be interesting to know more of the context of this newspaper story. Were the "Hill Billies" protesting a case during "Court-day"? Maybe they were just in town to blow off steam. Were they members of the local citizenry or from the surrounding region? Whatever the full story, it is clear that an early printed use of the term "hillbilly" contained negative connotations.

"A photograph taken in 1899, ... shows a large group of white people with three black servants out for an elaborate picnic in a wooded setting in Greenbrier County [West Virginia]. These prosperous people from Lewisburg most certainly knew the word hillbilly as a designation for social inferiors, yet someone of this group boldly hand-labeled the photograph 'Camp Hillbilly,' a voluntary association with a despised identity, a friendly jab at roughing it, and a sort of brag."[12]

A 1900 *New York Journal* article contained the definition: "a Hill-Billie is a free and untrammeled white citizen of Alabama, who lives in the hills, has no means to speak of, dresses as he can, talks as he pleases, drinks whiskey when he gets it, and fires off his revolver as the fancy takes him". [13]

These early examples of the word "hillbilly" clearly reflect the negative intent of the word usage as it flowed from vernacular slang into the wider print media. So where did the term originate?

The etymology of the word "hillbilly' is generally attributed to a Scottish/Celtic derivation: in its simplest form, "hill" referring to the highlands of Scotland and "billy" meaning "comrade" or "companion". Michael Montgomery attributes the term to settlers from Scotland and northern Ireland who were followers of King William III of Orange. Combining their native location and the diminutive of William, these Protestants took the name "Billy's Boys" or "Hillbillies".[14]

James F. Burns and James F. O'Leary wrote in the Lowell, Massachusetts Sun Times in a 2019 article, "The early Scots-Irish immigrants were Presbyterian but the Scottish church couldn't supply enough ministers to keep up with western expansion, allowing Methodists and Baptists to make huge inroads. But whatever stripe of Protestant they were, most Scots-Irish retained a hero-like worship of Good King Billy — King William III whose Protestant army won a huge victory in Ireland over his Catholic rival for the crown in 1690. The southern "Billy Boys" who populated the hill country of Appalachia were termed "hillbillies," intended as a derogatory term by some but celebrated by others. 'Hillbilly' is a derogatory term to some, but it's embraced by America's Scotch-Irish descendants". [15]

A problem with these historical word derivations is that there are hundreds of years between the European connections and the first documented usage of "hillbilly" in America. So the etymology is somewhat questionable. Whatever the source for "hillbilly", once its use began in the United States, it almost immediately took on a negative slang meaning.

Although the intent of this book is to analyze and discuss the term "hillbilly", it may add some context to briefly mention a couple other terms of similar usage. These monikers can take on different connotations just like hillbilly can. And although they generally have a negative implication, they are also sometimes used with a positive intent, particularly when they are used among members of like circumstances. Surprisingly, these terms also seem to have at least some link to Celtic derivation.

The term "redneck" came to popular use in the United States during the 20th century. It often refers to poor, White southerners, but has come to be used as a reference to anyone who comes from a rural or farming background. Its derivation in America most likely comes from the belief that someone who had to work outside would develop a sunburned or red neck, a portion of the anatomy not always covered. The implication is that there is something negative about working outside, an association that is both insulting and couched in class snobbery.

During the violent mine strikes in West Virginia in the early 1900s, striking workers sometimes wore red bandanas around their necks to identify themselves. The miners held this as a symbol of their strength and comradeship. Mine owners and their company strikebreakers and paramilitary enforcers used the term "redneck" to disparage the workers and their families. The mine workers fighting for improved working conditions were supported by Mary G. Harris "Mother" Jones, a union organizer. Mother Jones was an Irish immigrant who had fled the Great Famine as a child.[16]

The Celtic etymology of redneck may come from the Covenanters, lowland Scottish Protestants who fled to Ulster during persecution by the British Crown in the 17th century. These dissenters signed documents declaring that they supported a Presbyterian form of government and that they opposed the Church of England. They often signed these "covenants" in blood and like the much later American miners wore red scarves around their neck publicly declaring their dissent. Their "red badge of courage" earned them the moniker "redneck", which followed some of the Ulster-Scotch Presbyterians to America.[17]

In American culture, redneck is typically used in a demeaning manner, but as is often the case with epithets, some people have embraced it. Particularly in turn of the century labor unions and more recently in popular comedy and country music, the term and its associated social implications are almost celebrated.[18]

"Cracker" most often refers to a poor, White southerner and depending on the namer and the namee, has racial overtones. Cracker has a compelling duality in that it can be perceived as a blatant insult or a badge of honor. In this country, the term may have derived from association with "whip-cracker", referring to someone who uses a whip on livestock or unfortunately, people. Again, the word takes on implications of rural *vs.* urban and class and racial distinctions.

There is evidence that cracker has a distinct derivation from the Gaelic word "craic", meaning talk or conversation, which was probably borrowed from the Shakespearian English "craker". Shakespeare used the term to describe someone who talked too much: "What craker is this same that deafs our ears with this abundance of superfluous breath?"[19]

In his comprehensive book *Down in the Holler*[20], Vance Randolph defines hillbilly as "A derisive name for the mountaineer, as contrasted with the valley-farmer and the city-dweller". He then lists no less than twenty colorful synonyms.

A list of similar, stereotyping, name calling epithets might include: blackmouth, gringo, peckerwood, rube, yokel, backwoodsman, hick, bumpkin, clodhopper, hayseed, ridge runner. You get the idea. All these words can insult or inspire comradeship and identity. But here, we will concentrate on the hillbilly in all his or her positive and negative traits.

Based on these theories of word derivation, use of the term hillbilly appears to have arisen as a more affectionate term; a name conferring friendship, a common history and perhaps a common religious and political bent. The word may have conveyed elements of joking banter between people with similar socio-economic position or was used to provide a feeling of comradeship among people in difficult situations.

But as hillbilly entered more mainstream usage, it immediately took on a negative connotation. As its use spread, it was co-opted from the ownership of its originators and used to disparage. Frequently used in a supposedly comic context, hillbilly still carried a sting, conveyed by a group perceiving itself as superior on a group seen as inferior. Hillbillies became "the others", frowned upon as uneducated, simple, crude, even dangerous.

The Ozarks as a region has many claims for a positive image. It has always been admired for its environmental beauty, its expansive forests, its biodiversity and its springs, rivers and lakes. Native Americans lived communally in the geographic region roughly outlined between the Missouri, Arkansas, Neosho and Mississippi Rivers. The earliest known inhabitants the Bluffdwellers took advantage of the rock shelters to create their homes along the alluvial terraces of the free flowing streams. They hunted and foraged the diverse ecosystems of the Ozarks highlands. Later, the Osage made this region their home, temporarily ruling over the hills, valleys and prairies.

Settlers of European origin took advantage of the Ozarks' resources, primarily furs, timber and lead deposits. But settlement of the region was slow. Much of the Ozarks was bypassed during the American western expansion for more accessible or tillable land. Particularly in the Ozarks highlands of northern Arkansas and southern Missouri, settlement consisted largely of isolated, subsistence farmsteads.

*Butler Hollow, Barry County Missouri*

Early documenters of the Ozarks were not often kind about the inhabitants of these verdant, well-watered hills. Henry Rowe Schoolcraft made a trip through the region in 1818-1819 and published his impressions of the inhabitants.

"In manners, morals, customs, dress, contempt of labor and hospitality, the state of society is not essentially different from that which exists among the savages. Schools, religion, and learning, are alike unknown. Hunting is the principal, the most honourable, and the most profitable employment. To excel in the chase procures fame, and a man's reputation is measured by his skill as a marksman, his agility and strength in killing game, and his patient endurance and contempt of the hardships of the hunter's life. They are, consequently, a hardy, brave, independent people, rude in appearance, frank and generous, travel without baggage, and can subsist anywhere in the woods and would form the most efficient military corps in frontier warfare which can possibly exist. Ready trained, they require no discipline, inured to danger, and perfect in the use of the rifle. Their system of life is, in fact, one continued scene of camp-service. Their habitations are not always permanent, having little which is valuable, or loved, to rivet their affections to any one spot, and nothing which is venerated, but what they can carry with them; they frequently change residence, travelling where game is more abundant."[21]

So in one of the earliest written publications about the Ozarks region, Schoolcraft creates an impression that is both critical and perhaps grudgingly admiring of the region's mountain man. It must be mentioned that Schoolcraft and his companion, Levi Pettibone, struggled to survive in this vast wilderness and often relied on both the hospitality and generosity of the "savages" they encountered. This duality in the descriptions and impressions of the hill people would occur frequently in publications by visitors to the Ozarks hill country throughout the nineteenth and early twentieth centuries. These reports were almost always produced by outsiders who brought their lack of experience, their prejudices and their preconceived notions about Ozarkers into their accounts. Some of the stories were very critical, some were admiring and most contained elements of disdain and respect.

George W. Featherstonhaugh, a British-American and first U.S. geologist, was assigned to explore portions of the Louisiana Purchase in 1834. His comments on his experiences in northern Arkansas were mostly negative regarding the inhabitants of the frontier Ozarks. Featherstonhaugh criticized nearly every trait of the people he encountered including their homes, food, dress, work ethic and intelligence.[22] Like Schoolcraft, Featherstonhaugh did not complain about all those he met in his journeys, but he disparaged many of the same people who tried their best to be hospitable. In his lengthy report,[23] *Excursion Through the Slave States* he carps about one such accommodation near the headwaters of the Little Red River:

"Hornby was a squalid, half-negro looking, piratical ruffian from Louisiana, living in a wretched, filthy cabin, with a wife to match, and a Caliban-looking negress and her two children, who were his slaves. This fellow never opened his mouth without uttering execrations of the worst kind. In this den, which had only one beastly room, we were obliged to stay and suffer the low conversation of this horrid fellow. Some bits of filthy fried pork, and a detestable beverage they were pleased to call coffee, were set on a broken dirty table at which, by the light of a nasty little tin lamp, into which Madame Hornby, after helping herself to the pork, poured some of its grease, we all, *tutti quanti*, sat on two lame benches. We passed a most disgusting night, the whole party lying down on the floor; and, from the appearance of every thing around me, I should certainly, if I had been alone, have expected an attempt on my life. A place better fitted for the nefarious practices of such a set of desperate-looking human beings I have never seen."

Frederick Gerstaecker, a young German adventurer, spent time in Arkansas from 1837 to 1843. In his book, *Wild Sports in the Far West*, he criticized the violent lifestyle of some of the Ozarkers he encountered, but then proceeded to extol a romanticized version of the mountain man as a true natural being living in commune with his environment. "I have traversed the State [Arkansas] in all directions, and met with as honest and upright people as are to be found in any part of the Union." [24]

*Cover of Gerstaeker's chronicle*

In the late 1850s, Irish Catholic priest Father John Joseph Hogan from St. Louis traveled to southern Missouri in search of land for a Catholic Irish colony. Although not published until 1892, Hogan presented a very positive image of the few settlers he encountered in his journey through Missouri's Oregon and Ripley counties.

"In keeping with these scenes were the simple, quiet ways of the early settlers of southern Missouri, who were mostly from

North Carolina and Tennessee, and of whom much may be said in praise. They were kindhearted, honest, sincere and sociable. No stranger ever traveled amongst them without feeling his heart warmed with the fullest conviction, that, if worthy his presence gave them pleasure, that he was treated to the best they had or could afford, and that his person, money and property were safe and sacred in their keeping. Vice was little known amongst them. Intemperance was nowhere observable, although they usually took as a matter of course, their morning dram, or a drop with a friend, from a keg of the best, distilled by themselves or by some neighbor willing to share or barter on accommodating terms. Every one smoked, men and women, young and old. The weed grew abundantly, and was usually the best tended patch of crop on the place. There was no need of manufactured tobacco or of fancy pipes. Home grown and home manufacture found favor. Corncob pipes were easily made, and for pipe stems cane was abundant. It grew along the streams and by the water's side. The maidens and swains married young, usually before twenty, often at sixteen and their married life was remarkably virtuous and happy. The marriage dowry was usually a one room log house. The young man was fortuned by his father with a yoke of oxen and a plow. The bride was dowered by her mother with wealth of homespun dresses and household fabrics of like man-ufacture. Timber from a neighboring sawmill was easily framed into a variety of articles of household furniture, and the eyes of the young couple were none the less delighted with it, for be-ing pure of veneer or varnish, of which their rural surroundings gave them no knowledge whatever. Uncle Sam had given them a homestead of three hundred and twenty acres, at twelve and a half cents per acre. There was no reason in the world why they should not be happy. Moreover, the young wife had been taught by her mother to knit, spin, weave and sew. The young husband had been taught by his father to tend sheep and cattle, and to cul-tivate cotton and corn. The education of husband and wife could be depended upon to procure them a living. The plow cultivated plots and furrows in the field. The wheel and loom wrought fab-rics at home. There was no need of the merchant's ship, bringing goods from afar. No need of town fashions, or of store clothes.

Willing hands and humble hearts made the one-room log cabin a sacred place and a happy home."[25]

Hogan's rosy description of Ozarks life and Gerstaecker's penchant for praising the hillfolk as genuine examples of common, rugged natives unspoiled by an urban, industrialized society would take root in the observations of chroniclers following the Civil War and well into the twentieth century. Reaction against the ills of urban growth and industrialization and a yearning for a more pastoral, simple life gained considerable interest through movements like Arcadianism, the Arts and Crafts Movement and the Country Life Movement. In 1908, President Theodore Roosevelt appointed a Commission on Country Life to preserve traditional rural lifestyles while improving the circumstances of the then still highly agrarian rural population. The positive portrayals of Ozarks mountain life at least brought admiration for the perceived benefits of rural life. How much they changed perceptions of the people living in the mountainous regions of Missouri and Arkansas may be disputable.

Perhaps the most enduring presentation of positive Ozarks life and the hillbilly image came from Harold Bell Wright's publication of *The Shepherd of the Hills* in 1907. Although Wright's work has been criticized for its literary value, there is no doubt that *The Shepherd of the Hills* was and is extremely popular. And this book deserves considerable credit for generating interest in the Ozarks and helping create a regional tourism boom that has lasted for well over one hundred years.

Wright's story is full of characters that embody both sides of the hillbilly image, from the violence of Wash Gibbs and the Bald Knobbers to the steady strength of Aunt Molly and Old Matt. The portrayal of the Ozarks mountain people was romanticized and appealed to a wide readership who seemed to long for a simpler, rustic existence. Wright's novel went a long way toward presenting a positive image of the Ozarks hillfolk and perhaps is one of the best examples of a constructive depiction of the hillbilly, although to these writers' knowledge, Wright never used that term.

Early on, the concept of the hillbilly persona was coopted by both outlanders and natives. Since the early 1800s, the hillbilly character has been used in a comic presentation. The stereotype has been portrayed as a complete rube, a knowledgeable rustic and a sly fox who gets one up on the naïve city feller. The comedic hillbilly portrayals were popularized by the Southwestern humorists.

In the 1830-40s, Charles Fenton Mercer Noland published several short stories in the New York weekly magazine *Spirit of the Times* about a fictional backwoods character, Pete Whetstone. A Batesville, Arkansas lawyer, Noland wrote of Whetstone's adventures with bear hunting, horse racing, country dances and other rustic pursuits. Noland's hillbilly character often winds up in a setting where comic results unfold. The fictional Whetstone is endowed with both positive and negative characteristics.

In his book *Arkansas/Arkansaw*, Brooks Blevins identifies another story published in the *Spirit of the Times* in 1841 written by Thomas Bangs Thorpe, "The Big Bear of Arkansas", as "the most famous example of southwestern humor". [26] In "Big Bear", the protagonist Jim Doggett relates a bear hunting story to a group of passengers on a Mississippi steamboat. The tale includes elements of backwoods braggadocio, hill country language, and hunting prowess. Doggett is characterized as both a romanticized rustic hero and a coarse outlier from the more "civilized" society.

One of the most lasting personalities of Southwestern humor and for that matter the hillbilly stereotype in general, is the Arkansas Traveler. Its origin is generally attributed to a tale developed and propagated in 1840 by Arkansas politician Colonel Sanford C. Faulkner. Albert Pike may also deserve some credit for origins of the tale in stories he wrote in *Letters from Arkansas* in 1833.

The tale involves an urbane gentleman traveling into the backwoods of Arkansas (probably the Boston Mountains), who encounters a mountain man playing his fiddle outside his crude home. A dialogue ensues with the fiddler providing comedic responses to the traveler's inquiries.

The Traveler tale spawned multiple versions that all provided a wry presentation of the dual nature of the hillbilly. The homespun fiddler seems on the surface to be somewhat dense and argumentative. Yet as the repartee continues between the two, it becomes clear that the hillsman may indeed achieve the upper hand over the sophisticate.

The Arkansas Traveler image became so popular that it generated paintings, a play and a popular fiddle tune. The citizens of Arkansas have never been quite sure what to do with the Traveler. The story has been both honored and rejected. Arkansas has granted "Arkansas Traveler Certificates" to visiting dignitaries since 1941. Little Rock's baseball team has carried the name Arkansas Travelers since 1895. The University of Arkansas student newspaper is still called the *Arkansas Traveler*. [27]

The Arkansaw Traveller Folk Theater operated as a tourist attraction near Hardy, Arkansas starting in 1968. With performances lasting for several years, the production presented a version of the Traveler tale along with traditional and popular Ozarks folk music.

*Currier & Ives print of Edward Payson Washbourne's painting Arkansas Traveler; circa 1870*

Opie Read worked as a newspaperman and writer for several years in the late 1800s and early 1900s. Originally from Tennessee, he served as city editor of the *Arkansas Democrat* and *Arkansas Gazette* out of Little Rock. Read's newspaper experiences and travels around the South resulted in extensive material for his fictional writing, including *The Arkansaw Traveler*, a magazine distributed nationally from 1882 to 1893.

Opie Read certainly knew the city and town characters of his time, but his actual knowledge of hillfolk may be somewhat suspect. He often portrayed the mountain people of northern Arkansas in a comic light. He wasn't necessarily negative in these fictional characterizations, but his depictions do seem to lack some authenticity. Read's extensive use of rural dialect seems stilted.

In his many novels and short stories, Read presented a mixed view of the Ozarks (and the postbellum South) that reached a significant American audience. His blend of praise and scorn can be seen in the following excerpt from *Up Terrapin River*:[28]

"Terrapin River flows through the northern part of Arkansas. It is a small stream, winding its way among hills, which here with graceful slope, and there with rugged brows, overlook the smooth and gliding water. The water, when the current is not swollen, is so clear that the stream suggests the blended flow of countless dewdrops. The brooks that flow into Terrapin River seem to float down sun-beams, gathered in the hill-tops. Up the 'hollow', the cow-bell's mellow clang floats away in slowly dying echo. The country through which Upper Terrapin River flows is slow of agricultural development.

The rankest of corn grows in the 'bottoms', and on the uplands the passing breezes steal the fragrance of the mellowest of horse-apples. The people, the most of them at least, are rude of speech. To them the smooth sentences of culture are as over-ripe strawberries — unfit for use. The popular estimate of a man's mental strength in this neighborhood is based upon the roughness of his expressions. There are schools, but, save in the winter, they are ill attended, for the children, so soon as they are old enough to study, are also large enough to lend important aid to the cultivation of the crops. Among those people there are many peculiar characters."

Opie Read's prolific output certainly had some influence on the image of the Ozarks people. He could be sympathetic, but also derogatory. To be fair, he was usually writing fiction and he often intended to be humorous. But his work does seem to impart an "otherness" to his fictional characters. Like so many writers of the nineteenth century, Read created a representation that was entertaining, but not always accurate.

The cursory view of the hillbilly image presented in this chapter is an attempt to provide a synopsis of the derivation of the term, some historical context for its origins and development, and some of the roots and impact of its dual nature in our society. The following chapters will round out how the hillbilly has come to be perceived, how the hillbilly image has been used in our culture, and how the term can carry both negative and positive implications.

The wide range of hillbilly images that have been promulgated through popular arts and media will be examined. Along the way, suggestions on how the image can be seen in a more positive light are advocated and examples provided of real people who exemplify these traits and accept if not embrace the term. Hillbilly will never lose its sting of belittlement, but there is an alternate view that perhaps can reveal what some Ozarkers have always known — the hillbilly has many constructive traits worn under that rough exterior.

# Chapter 2

## Mountaineers and Hillbillies

*Joseph Philibert* was not a mountaineer by birth, but he certainly lived an existence that mirrors, at least to some degree, the early perceptions of the hillbilly image.

Philibert, of French descent, born in 1802 in St. Louis, spent some of his early years living with Native Americans along the Mississippi River near St. Genevieve. He became acquainted with an Indian trader William Gillis. From 1822 to 1831 Philibert worked with Gillis at a trading post operation called Delaware Town along the James River deep in the Ozarks highlands.

Delaware Town was a semi-permanent home for members of the Delaware, Wea, Piankenshaw and Peoria tribes who lived in the area about fourteen miles south of the present location of Springfield (Springfield was founded in 1831). Joseph Philibert worked for Gillis in several capacities: as a clerk at his trading post, trading manufactured goods for furs with the Indians, and transporting wares back and forth across the practically nonexistent wagon road known as Old Piney Road of southern Missouri.

Philibert later described the Gillis residence at Delaware Town.

"It was a one story hewed log house known as a double house with an entry in between. The south room was the kitchen, the north room was the Gillis' room. A door from each room opened into the open entry and one door on the west side of the kitchen opening to the outside. One window in the east side of Gillis' room and a chimney at each end of the house." [29] Today this kind of building would be called a "dogtrot" cabin and was a fairly common dwelling for those of substantial means in the early Ozarks.

Philibert learned to speak some of the Indian languages and developed an understanding of their way of life, although the Amerinds he encountered had been significantly influenced by Europeans.

By 1833, Philibert had left Gillis' employ and homesteaded thirty-one acres at the junction of the James and White Rivers. The same year he married sixteen-year-old Peninah Yoachum of the legendary silver dollar Yoachums. Philibert expanded his homestead, continuing to trade with the local settlers and Indians still in the area.

In 1870, Joseph Philibert gave testimony in a court case involving the will of William Gillis. Gillis had fathered several children including some by Indian women. Two of Gillis' granddaughters successfully contested his will and ultimately received a share of Gillis' estate.

In Joseph's testimony he revealed some aspects of his life at the mouth of the James River saying he had several health problems including "liver complaint" and "neuralgia in the head". Philibert said he had "nearly or quite" lost sight in his right eye.

During his deposition for the Gillis case, Philibert was asked how he had been affected by the Civil War. Joseph replied:

"[I was] very much disturbed by the late rebellion while living at the mouth of James Fork of White River. I was disturbed some of course by Secesh and Union men both. The rebels came to kill me and the Union men took my corn, flour, bacon, hay and everything. The Secesh took upwards of $900 in gold." [30] After a long life in the wilds of the Ozark Mountains, Joseph Philibert died at his home on the river in 1884.

In 1948, Ben and Betty Loftin purchased 640 acres of land where the James River flowed into the White. The Loftin farm, encompassing the original Philibert homestead, included large areas of fertile bottomland, a natural pond, a high peninsula between the White and James and forested ridgelines. The bottomland was on high terraces that flooded infrequently. With his father and brother, Ben grew corn and hay and ran Herefords on the pastures. The Loftins also raised hogs and kept sheep which they sheared for wool.

From 1951 to 1956, excavations were performed at the Loftin farm as part of the project to evaluate archaeological sites within the boundaries of the coming Table Rock Lake project. Significant findings during these digs included evidence of a possible ceremonial mound and the remains of at least five Indian dwellings. There was also material uncovered indicating the presence of the homestead and possible trading post established here in 1833 by Joseph Philibert.

In 1956, most of the Loftin farm was sold through eminent domain to the Corps of Engineers for the coming Table Rock Lake. Today, the Philibert and Loftin sites are drowned beneath the water of Table Rock. The Loftins relocated to a new farm near Reeds Spring. When asked about losing his home on the river, Ben said, "It makes me mad every time I go down there." [31]

A reminder of the historical significance of the site once home to Joseph Philibert is the Corps Park on the east side of the James River arm of Table Rock called Joe Bald Park. Rising above the area are three knobs, Little Joe Bald, Big Joe Bald and Naked Joe Bald.[32]

Chapter 1 explored some of the sources and derivations of the term hillbilly and the associated image. With roots in the ancient Celtic culture, many of the people who initially settled and populated the Ozarks mountain region were courageous, independent trailblazers who needed particular skills to establish and maintain their lives in the isolated hills and hollows. Their skill sets did not require learned, cultured manners; they required primitive, wild lore.

Early observers and documenters of the hillfolk, primarily outlanders, were frequently critical of the mountain people's lifestyle. They often only begrudgingly recognized some of their positive traits. These chroniclers often failed to acknowledge the connection between the pioneers' mode of living and the requirements of existing in a demanding, difficult environment.

As the accounts of Ozarks life filtered into the outside world, the perception of a wild, uncouth populace took hold.

Throughout most of the nineteenth century, descriptions of the folk living in the mountainous Ozarks country were full of either comic or outright insulting characterizations. But these descriptions often either ignored or downplayed the traits required to settle and sustain a life in the rough Ozark hills.

In the first half of the nineteenth century, pioneers slowly moved deeper and deeper into the hills and hollows of southern Missouri and northern Arkansas. Some came up the wild, free flowing rivers of the region. Others blazed or followed rough wagon roads. Settlements grew up along the rivers and eventually towns rose, particularly in the prairie and lowland regions. Many of these towns like Springfield, Fayetteville and Batesville (originally Poke Bayou) evolved like towns in other frontier regions of the United States.

But some of the settlers moving in from the eastern mountains chose to establish their new homes in the more isolated environs. Land was available for squatter's rights or at bargain prices. Perhaps they picked these places because the opportunities for hunting were better. Or maybe they just preferred a life that was more independent and isolated. Intentionally or not, these insular people had to rely on their own skills and attributes to sustain their way of life. Cut off from most outside influence, they retained old ways of doing things that had worked for centuries and saw no reason to change.

*Tommie Redfearn- expert Ozarks sorghum maker*

Ozarkers cling close to the land. The land provides. Existence in the backwoods of the Ozarks relied on hunting, trapping, fishing, foraging and farming. The more successful farmers were in the richer bottomlands. But even along the rocky hillsides, a family could establish a vegetable garden, plant a small corn crop, raise a cow or two, tend chickens, and produce free range hogs.

This was not an easy life. It required hard work and commitment. The stereotype of the "lazy hillbilly" belies the fact that if you were going to make it in the Ozarks, you were going to have to work hard. Toil did not always guarantee success and the rewards of scratching out an existence were few.

The hillbilly mountaineer had to have certain traits to sustain life in the woods. Hunting, trapping and fishing skills were highly valuable and regarded. Knowledge of the natural world and its plants and animals could make the difference between life and death. Farming practices were often less than ideal, but it still took lots of hard work and commitment to produce and preserve a crop.

The mountain hillbilly's social life revolved primarily around the family. Many of the pioneers moving into the Ozarks came with large family groups. A large family was an asset for a subsistence existence on the land. The family and close neighbors (if there were any) had to work together to succeed. Outside help was just not going to come and was probably not welcomed anyway.

Religion did play a role in the mountain people's lives. Early on, there were very few churches in the hill country. Certainly some families, usually of a Protestant bent, followed the tenets of a Christian life. But some of the first settlers were cut off from religion either by choice or circumstance. These unchurched people followed a code of morality based on their upbringing and their life situation. Outlanders tended to interpret this lack of religion as amorality. Perhaps a better description would be individual or group ethics based on primitive survival demands.

As the Ozarks became more populated toward the mid-nineteenth century, organized religion began to exert more influence. The towns and cities developed with congregations of traditional Protestants, particularly Baptists, Methodists and Cumberland Presbyterians. These branches of Christianity entered the mountain regions, too, but the congregations were smaller and individual sects and schism groups often formed in the isolated mountain enclaves.

Superstition was intertwined with nearly all elements of the mountain people's lives. Helen and Townsend Godsey reveal some of these beliefs in their book of classic photographs *Ozarks Mountain Folk These Were The Last*:[33]

"The 'bury hole' was dug by friends and relatives of the deceased and a grave was never left open overnight lest it claim another member of the family. As soon as possible after a death lest their bees die, too, or go away, a family member went from beehive to beehive telling the insects of the death. The clock was stopped, the mirrors, if they had any, were covered, cats put under a basket or tub and the pillow of the deceased carefully opened in hopes of finding an angel crown."

Vance Randolph collected hundreds of superstitious beliefs from throughout the Ozarks and published them in his *Ozark Superstitions*. In the book's introduction, in his usual analytical approach, Randolph presents his opinion about the meaning of superstition for the hillfolk:[34]

"Sophisticated visitors sometimes regard the 'hillbilly' as a simple child of nature, whose inmost thoughts and motivations may be read at a glance. Nothing could be farther from the truth. The hillman is secretive and sensitive beyond anything that the average city dweller can imagine, but he isn't simple. His mind moves in a tremendously involved system of signs and omens and esoteric auguries. He has little interest in the mental procedure that the moderns call science, and his ways of arranging data and evaluating evidence are very different from those currently favored in the world beyond the hilltops. The Ozark hillfolk have often been described as the most superstitious people in America. It is true that some of them have retained certain ancient notions which have been discarded and forgotten in more progressive sections of the United States."

Randolph adds to his dichotomous viewpoint writing:

"One might expect to find a definite negative correlation between superstition and intelligence, or at least between superstition and education, but this does not seem to be the case. Perhaps the most famous water witch who ever lived in southwest Missouri was a physician, a graduate of Washington University, and a man of really extraordinary attainments. One

64

of the most credulous and superstitious hillmen I ever knew was intelligent enough to learn surveying and had sufficient book learning to enable him to teach the district school with unprecedented success." [35]

*Ozark Superstitions* compiles a wide range of superstitions, omens, tales and stories associated with the region covering topics including weather signs, mountain medicine, courtship, and death. The beliefs run the gamut from heartwarming to ridiculous to frightening. The following excerpts illustrate how these superstitions intersected with the mountain folks' lives:

"Some years ago a prominent Ozark farmer suffered from hiccoughs, which continued for many days, so that his life was endangered. One yarb doctor said that if the man would just grind up some white beans, mix the resulting powder with vinegar, and take a teaspoonful every thirty minutes, he would stop hiccoughing within twenty-four hours—this was tried without any results. Other local healers contended that a big dose of dill tea, or tea made of the inner lining of a chicken gizzard, would cure hiccoughs almost immediately. An old woman from Rocky Comfort, Missouri, wrote the man's doctor suggesting that he 'drench' the patient with sweet milk and black-pepper tea. A poultice of raw potatoes, fastened tightly across the abdomen, was also highly recommended. An amateur herbalist at Pineville, Missouri, told me that a tonic mixture of whisky, tansy, and ragweed leaves was indicated in all such cases; 'I take it every day myself, 'said he,' an' it agrees with me fine. I ain't had the hiccoughs but once in fourteen years.'" [36]

"In some sections of Arkansas, the girls 'set a dumb supper,' by making a pone of cornmeal and salt, in complete silence. Each girl must take her turn at stirring the meal, each must shift the pone as it bakes; each must place a piece of bread on her own plate, and another on the plate next to hers at the table. When this is done, the girls open the doors and windows, then sit down silently and bow their heads. All during the baking, the wind has grown stronger, and by this time there should be a regular gale blowing through the house. Often the lights are blown out. The phantom husbands are supposed to enter in silence. Each girl is supposed to recognize the man who sits down beside her. If she sees nobody, it means she will never marry. If she sees a black figure, without recognizable features, it means that she will die within a year. Many people still take this business seriously enough to forbid their daughters to trifle with it. Some parents say it ain't Christian and smells of witchcraft, while others object to such foolishness because it sometimes frightens nervous girls into hysteria." [37]

Mary Elizabeth Mahnkey related an eerie story about "dumb suppers" in the *White River Leader* newspaper edition of January 4, 1934. In this tale, a young girl participates in a dumb supper, laying a unique knife at the place setting for her intended. Eventually she marries a stranger and they appear to be happy. When the woman reveals the story of the conjuring to her husband, he confronts her saying, "And you are the one. You are that witch. That night I walked through hell." He stabs his bride fatally with the same knife she had set out at the fateful "supper".[38]

Superstition played an important role in the lives of the mountain folk and certainly added to the image of the hillbilly persona as backward and foolish. But these beliefs also added to the mystique and lore of the Ozarks hill people. These traits give them a uniqueness and cultural characteristic that can be interesting and even endearing.

*A "witch peg"*

Medical care for the Ozarker was a conglomeration of home remedies, herbal medicine, superstition and the occasional "professional" doctor. The availability of physicians has always been a problem in the mountain country. The early settlers most often relied on their own skills as healers, as they did for almost every other need.

Some of the home remedies were based on old tried and true herbal treatments that were passed down through generations. Others were learned from Native Americans. Many were based on superstition. Even the cures practiced by some doctors, when they were available, were often crude and sometimes did more harm than good.

Isolation, lack of education and sheer necessity led to the acceptance of "healers" of many stripes. Perhaps the most common was the midwife or "granny woman". These women were valued in the mountain country and usually performed their function well. They followed skill sets often handed down in their family. They filled a necessary role for the community, assisting with childbirth, treating female problems and providing general medical care and advice. Mid-wifery played an important role in the Ozarks mountain enclaves and is still practiced today.

The use of medicinal plants and herbs was common in the Ozarks. The "yarb doctor" was often a woman, but men also sought out, cultivated, prepared and administered herbal remedies. Many of these remedies had true value, while others were potentially harmful or at best worthless. The yarb doctor protected her sources of plants and her recipes. Secret plots of ginseng and echinacea were carefully tended and safe guarded.

Sometimes added to home cures were the nostrums available from traveling medicine shows or at the nearest general store. These patent medicines were occasionally of some use, but often provided little or no medical value.

Otto Rayburn writes:

"Mrs. May Kennedy McCord of Springfield, Missouri says that in the old Ozarks, granny-woman was the popular name for mid-wife, but that she was sometimes called a 'medicine woman' if she gathered herbs and doctored with them. Her garden usually contained digitalis, golden seal, belladonna, lobelia, sage, henna, rhubarb, and many others. She collected May apples, blood root, wild cherry and numerous other herbs from the woods."[39]

While the granny woman and yarb doctor performed duties based on experience and mostly tried and true methods, the power doctor or "goomer" practiced healing based on assumed psychic or religious powers. The power doctor's interventions were clearly rooted in superstition or spiritual belief. However, despite their lack of scientific basis, these ministrations often had a placebo effect. If the patients and the healer thought they would work, sometimes they did work.

At the extreme end of Ozarks medical practitioners were the witches. Although usually, but not always, females, the witch could play both negative and positive roles. Belief in witchcraft has a long history and can be associated with ancient Celtic ritual, Christian teaching and backcountry superstition.

One woman who was sometimes identified as a "witch" was Miss Jean Wallace, more affectionately known as the "mountain maid". Miss Jean made her home in a rough cabin in a very isolated location near Roaring River in Barry County, Missouri. She homesteaded 160 acres single-handedly around 1892 and lived out her life there until her death in 1940.

The Mountain Maid possessed "special powers" from an early age. She did not necessarily promote her abilities, but local folk came to know she could locate lost items and foretell some events. As she aged, Jean lived a difficult existence, but chose to stay in her rough abode. In the 1930s, young men from Roaring River's CCC camp befriended her and assisted her needs. The mountain maid lost her life when her cabin burned in 1940.

Miss Jean said of her abilities, "I belong to a race of people that can see. My great-grandfather, a Wallace, was the greatest seer in Scotland. He could describe exactly how a man was dressed, even if he was as far off as India. The gift was handed down to me."[40]

*Miss Jean Wallace "The Mountain Maid"*

In his typically thorough and forthright manner, Vance Randolph relates a comprehensive review of Ozarks witchcraft in *Ozark Magic and Folklore*. The witch stories he relates are fantastic and often horrible.[41]

"In 1924 some witchcraft material which came to my attention seemed so extraordinary that I suspected my friends were greening me — *greening* is a dialect word which means spoofing. It was only after checking and double-checking these tales, and getting almost identical items from different people in widely separated sections of the hill country, that I began to realize the extent to which superstition still flourished in this region."

"Here is another old fireside tale, current in the late eighties. I got this particular version from Clarence Sharp, who heard it near Dutch Mills, Arkansas. The story goes that a hillman was just falling asleep when a pretty girl appeared with a bridle in her hand. In a twinkling she turned the poor fellow into a pony, leaped on his back, and rode him wildly through the woods. Later on she hitched him at the mouth of a cave, and he saw a group of 'furriners' carrying big sacks of money into the cavern. Finally she rode him back home, and he woke up next morning all tired out and brier-scratched. This happened night after night, and the hillman consulted a famous witch master. The witch master advised him to mark the tree to which he was tied at night, so that he could find it again in the daytime. Then, said the witch master, it would be an easy matter to waylay the witch and kill her with a silver bullet, and afterwards they could get the treasure in the cave.

So the next night, being transformed into a horse, the hill-man 'drapped as many drappin's' as he could to mark the place and started in to chaw a big blaze on the sapling to which he was tied. 'I chawed an' I chawed,' he said, 'an' all of a sudden come a hell of a noise an' a big flash o' light. Then I heered a lot o' hollerin', an' it sounded like my old woman was a'doin' the hollerin'. Quick as a wink I seen I was home again, an' it seemed like' — here the Hillman stole a furtive glance at his wife, who sat stolidly smoking by the fireplace — 'it seemed like I'd went an' benastied the bed-blankets, an' dang near bit the old wom-an's leg off!'"[42]

The Ozarks has always been blessed with plenty of water and springs are bountiful. The karst topography of the Ozark Highlands produces extensive underground caverns and water flows into and out of the rocky terrain. As water passes over limestone and dolomite, it produces carbonic acid which cor-rodes the stony Ozark foundation. This action results in con-siderable mineral content in the region's aquifers. The resultant mineral springs have attracted humans for thousands of years.

Devil's Pool at what is now Big Cedar Lodge was once con-sidered a sacred pool by the Osage who called it Spirit Pool for its healing powers. Similar mineral springs exist throughout the region. Many of these springs were touted for their healing abil-ity. Perhaps the best known of these medicinal springs are in the town of Eureka Springs, Arkansas.

Situated along a deep ravine, the springs of Eureka were re-portedly discovered by Dr. Alvah Jackson in 1856. Believing the many springs in the area had healing power, Jackson marketed the water as "Dr. Jackson's Eye Water" and opened "Dr. Jackson's Cave Hospital". Word of Jackson's medicinal waters spread and soon people came to partake and families took up residence near the springs.

Eureka Springs was founded in 1879 and the town grew rapidly. The city boomed with homes, saloons and hotels. Health tourism took off and Eureka had a population of nearly 4000 by 1880. The influx of wealthy cure seekers established a town based primarily on tourism. Over the years, Eureka Springs' fortunes waxed and waned, sensitive to the vagaries of medical practices, tourism fluctuations and economic trends.

Eureka's uniqueness not only comes from its many springs, unusual terrain, and resultant building styles, it is a town composed of outlanders. It doesn't have the symbolic images of isolation, backwardness and primitiveness that are often yoked to small Ozarks towns.

In recent years, Eureka Springs has drawn a very diverse population (although not racially diverse). The town has attracted and promotes artists and writers, traditionalistic Christians, and a significant lesbian and gay community. These diverse factions do create some dissention, but surprisingly, the town seems to manage fine, if not prosper.[43]

Perhaps this is why Eureka has avoided the "hillbilly" image. Its establishment, its development, its people and its image is somehow different than most other mountain communities. Whether it is fair or not, Eureka Springs can be viewed as a unique, beautiful outlier in a broad Ozarkian tableau.

Descriptions of the land and life in the Ozarks highlands can be gleaned from family histories as told by their descendants. These families came into the mountains in the first half of the 19th century and established a lineage and lore that exists to the present.

Ruth Henson Asher related the following story in the "White River Valley Historical Quarterly" in 1966.[44]

"Elder Thomas Henson was a circuit riding minister of the Baptist Church of Christ being ordained in Rutherford County, Tennessee. He came to the territory of Southwest Missouri in the early 1830s with his Bible, church papers, his horse, and chopping axe. He rode about the trails preaching, marrying and burying folks. Mostly the trails followed the streams. He came from southern Illinois, (Morgan County). It is a matter of record of his having performed the marriage ceremony for Permelia Yokum and Joseph Philbert in 1883[45]. He served in the War of 1812 from Morgan County, Illinois.

In 1835 he brought his family of 12 through St. Louis and down the much worn trail to Springfield. They came by oxen drawn cart with most of the children walking. Rebecca said there was one general store at that time in Springfield. The family bought, among other things, an iron pot for cooking.

Traveling with the Hensons were the John Barnett Williams and Elijah McLain Todd families. The Williams family was from Franklin, Simpson County, Kentucky. John B. Williams was a miller by trade and set up the first grist mill [elsewhere described as a "powder mill"] west of the Mississippi, at the mouth of Flat Creek where it meets the James, Mash Hollow at Cape Fair. Elder Henson must have picked out this homestead to bring his family to because of his scouting the land earlier. He settled on a very nice farm on Flat Creek a few miles above Cape Fair. A great grandson, John Asher, now owns the farm. One of the landmarks there is a large burr oak tree that Elder Henson's daughter, Rebecca, spoke of as being a good sized tree when they came to the farm in 1835.

Elder people of the area say that these now fine bottom farm lands were full of large trees at that early time and that it was a problem to clear the land. The large burr oak yet stands on the bank of Flat Creek below the cemetery where Thomas and his wife Rebecca are buried.

When Eli Asher, a great grandson, was a small boy, a man came (from Texas he thought) and cut names and dates on their rocks to mark them. Eli, now 80 years old, helped clean up the groves by cutting and piling the brush.

December 25, 1835 was given as the Henson date of arrival, that was the date of the marriage of a son, Zechariah and Armalie (Millie) Williams, born 1819, died 1877, a daughter of John B. Williams. These young people had fallen in love on the journey.

73

They settled above the Elder Henson place, just around the bend up Flat Creek, one mile south of the Barry County line. There they built and lived in a crude log cabin until the year 1850.

Elder Henson must have set up some sort of school on his farm for the children. His grandchildren remember going to a school in a building close to his home place and also near the now Cedar Bluff school house that still stands. No school being held there since 1951.

Once a year, on the fourth Sunday in September all the old friends of the district meet for an all day dinner on the grounds of the Old Cedar Bluff School. There we sing, tell old time school stories, recite poetry, take pictures and have a good time in general. 1965 marked the 20th year for this reunion. At one time it was District No. 2 in Stone County. One man, Lawrence Moore, 84 years old, sings the old song, "The Old School House on the Hill," from memory."

Ruth Henson Asher's daughter Sharon Asher Bennett still lives in the Cape Fair area above the confluence of Flat Creek and the James River. Her family's name is forever linked to the rich bottomland known as Asher Cane Bottom, now covered by the waters of Table Rock Lake.

The Henson/Asher family story is typical of the longevity of heritage and connection to the land the early settlers of the Ozark Mountains established. These folk found a way to make a solid life along the flowing streams and rugged ridges. They endured and prospered in a tough environment and through trying circumstances.

Green Berry Easley was one of the first pioneers to settle near what would become Eagle Rock. Born in Kentucky, Easley came to Boone County, Missouri and then to Barry County prior to 1840. Green Berry established a homestead at the mouth of Roaring River.

Easley built a substantial log and clapboard-sided house with large fireplaces in the kitchen and living room. Green and Eveline raised a large family and farmed the bottomland. An old trail crossed the White River at the Easley site. In 1860, Green Berry Easley was granted a license to operate a ferry on White River at the crossing of the Cassville and Carrolton road.

Green Berry acquired substantial land and is known to have loaned money to local people. His family toiled hard, working the land and running the ferry. It is believed that when he came from Boone County, he brought a supply of gold with him. Rumors of his assets and his anti-slavery views made Easley and his family a target of Civil war unrest and particularly marauding bushwhackers. It is likely that run-ins with bushwhackers resulted in the eventual death of Green in 1863 and his wife Eveline in 1864.[46]

The following story comes from Mrs. John Pascal Lee, the daughter-in-law of Hulda Easley, Green Berry's daughter:

"Hulda's father did not approve of slavery, and during the Civil War, freed his slaves. One slave, called "Black Mammy", cared for the children after their parents died, refusing to leave. Jayhawkers [who were] supposedly against slavery, but ransacked homes of both the North and South, came one day and took "Black Mammy" away. The children followed them to the White River, and the last they saw of her, she was riding behind one of the men on a horse as they boarded the ferry. Hulda's father owned the ferry, which was later sunk by cutting the cable, to prevent troops from the other side coming across."[47]

The Easley family persevered and proliferated throughout Barry County. There are still several Easleys and their descendants living in the upper White River Valley area.

A similar story of life for an Ozark "hillbilly" family was related by Jewel Farwell Hutchens.

Jewel Hutchens was born in 1921 on the Wire Road in Barry County. She was educated at Missouri State Teachers College (now Missouri State University) and Drury. As a girl, she visited Pineville to see the production of the 1939 movie "Jesse James". Her father supplied two horses for the movie and her brother was an extra. She met the actors Jane Darwell, Henry Fonda and Tyrone Power.

Jewel also remembers visiting the White River to camp at Eagle Rock and Easley Ford. A ferry boat had broken loose up river at Lewis Ford and wrecked at Easley Ford. The vessel was partially buried in the river bed and provided a swim platform for Jewel and her companions.

She moved to the Eagle Rock area in 1944 to teach school. Jewel married Ray Farwell in 1945 and lived until recently within view of the Eagle Rock Bridge over Table Rock Lake.

Ray Farwell's great-grandfather Albert Farwell bought several hundred acres on either side of the White River in 1858. He farmed the bottomland on both sides of the present site of the Eagle Rock Bridge. Albert grew corn and wheat and had an orchard.

Jewel Farwell relates the following about Albert Farwell:

"Ray's great-grandfather Albert went to take some supplies to Pea Ridge. They were having a battle there in 1862 in March. It was raining and he caught a bad cold. It went into pneumonia and he died. He only lived here not very long. He left five or six children and his widow.

So one night the bushwhackers came. She [Albert's widow] heard them out there. They were trying to get her cattle and horses. She was fighting them. They went clear off down to the river bank. They hit her in the head and she was laying down there. She finally came to and got back to the house.

When she did, the oldest daughter said, 'Well, we got to leave here. We don't have protection. No men with us.' What they did was mortgage the farm and got enough money to move into Cassville until the war was over.

This oldest daughter was a teacher. She started teaching when she was seventeen. She was the first woman from Barry County to graduate from the University of Missouri. She only lived to twenty-seven years old. She had typhoid. She never married. She felt like she was the one supposed to take care of the family. She taught long enough to pay off that mortgage."

The Farwells managed to keep most of their land in the family to the present. When Jewel moved to the farm in 1945, the home was located on the east side of the river. There was an older three room house on the property below the bridge crossing the White. This building was used as a construction office during erection of the Farwell Bridge in the late 30's. There was a hand-dug well at this site. Remnants of this well can still be seen below the Eagle Rock Park swimming beach at low water levels. The Farwell cemetery is still located within the Eagle Rock campground. At least two graves were moved from the bottomland to the existing cemetery during development of Table Rock.

Ray and Jewel farmed and ran cattle along the White River. Early on, there was no electricity at the farm. They drew water by hand from the old well. The Farwells used a gas refrigerator. Jewel liked to read books by the light of an Aladdin lamp. She enjoyed reading books like *Gone with the Wind* to Ray. Ray hunted and fished the river.

Route P, a gravel road, came up from the Arkansas line, crossed the White and traveled on to Eagle Rock and Cassville. This was a farm-to-market route serving area farms and providing access to the railheads. Local ranchers like Ray Farwell would drive herds of cattle and pigs to Cassville, Exeter or Eureka Springs. The cattle trail followed old Route F along Roaring River, a rough road crossing the stream several times.

In the mid-1950's, the Farwells were offered $139 an acre for their river bottomland along the White. Portions of their property would become Highway 86, approaches to the new Eagle Rock Bridge, the Eagle Rock Corps Park and Marina and Table Rock Lake.

Ray Farwell was not happy about losing portions of his land. He knew he would miss the river. Jewel relates "My husband didn't like the lake. He didn't like to fish in it. He loved to fish in that river. He'd get the best fish out of there- channel cat. Have you ever eaten channel cat? It's very good. Sometimes he had what he called a trot line and limb lines. You had to get up early because a lot of times they'd break loose. Good for breakfast."

When the White flooded in 1957, the Eagle Rock Bridge was covered with water. Ray ferried people across the deluge in his aluminum boat. After Table Rock was completed, Ray and Jewel continued to farm and ranch their remaining land. Ray eventually started an excavation business, taking advantage of the building boom occurring around the new reservoir. They also built and operated the Farwell Court lake resort. The Farwells raised their family along the White River and then Table Rock Lake. Their descendants continue to live and work in the Eagle Rock area — a landscape altered, but still retaining some of the qualities that attracted Albert Farwell 150 years ago.[48]

These stories of the Hensons, Easleys and Farwells give some insight into how the early mountaineers of the Ozarks region established successful lives and created a long line of determined, competent hillfolk. Their strength and doggedness belie the perceptions of Ozarkians as stereotypical lazy hillbillies. So where did these perceptions originate?

We have already briefly looked at some of the stereotyped images presented in the nineteenth century by the writings of outlanders like Schoolcraft and Featherstonhaugh and the portrayals in the "Big Bear" and "Arkansas Traveler" stories. Why did these concepts take hold and persist? What are the forces that supported and encouraged these portraits?

The writing of authors like Schoolcraft, Featherstonhaugh and Gerstaecker was mostly read by contemporaries in the academic, scientific and political arenas. It would take popular media to introduce the image of the Ozarks hillbilly to a wider audience. In the 1800s, that audience could best be reached through entertainment. One good example of the entertainment media was *Spirit of the Times*, a New York weekly newspaper originally published by William T. Porter.

The *Times* was a "sporting" newspaper and included items on horse racing, hunting, organized sports events and even theater productions. Its audience was upper class gentlemen of the northeast. Porter's newspaper magazine began circulation in 1831 and continued under other publishers throughout most of the 19th century. Early on, the *Spirit* included comical fictional stories of adventures and unique persons in the Old South. These tales were very popular and helped establish the genre of Southwestern humor.

Many of the southwest stories took place in the deep South, but Arkansas and even Missouri were not immune from the humorists' attention. In the Pete Whetstone tales, successful writer Charles Fenton Mercer Noland reveals perhaps some elements of his own colorful life. A Batesville lawyer, Noland penned several accounts of Whetstone's exploits around Arkansas which were published in the *Spirit of the Times*.

"Pete Whetstone, of Arkansas, was once travelling on horseback through the interior of the State, and called one evening to stay all night at a little log house near the road where entertainment and a post-office were kept. Two other strangers were there, and the mail rider rode up about dark. Supper being over, the mail carrier and the three gentlemen were invited into a small room furnished with a good fire and two beds, which were to accommodate the four persons for the night. The mail carrier was a little shabby, dirty, lousy-looking wretch, with whom none of the gentlemen liked the idea of sleeping. Pete Whetstone eyed him closely as he asked:

'Where do you sleep to-night, my lad?'

'I'll thleep with *you,* I reckon,' lisped the youth, 'or with one o' them other fellars, I don't care which.'

The other two gentlemen took the hint and occupied one of the beds together immediately, leaving the other bed and the confab to be enjoyed by Pete and the mail boy together as best they could. Pete and the boy both commenced hauling off their duds, and Pete getting in bed first, and wishing to get rid of sleeping with the boy, remarked very earnestly—'my friend, I'll tell you before hand, *I've got the Itch,* and you'd better not get in here with me, for the disease is *catching.*'

The boy, who was just getting in bed too, drawled out very cooly, 'wal I reckon that don't make a bit o' difference,-- I've had it now for nearly theven years,' and into bed he pitched along with Pete, who pitched out in as great a hurry as if he had waked up a hornet's nest in the bed. The other two gentlemen roared, and the mail boy, who had got peaceable possession of a bed to himself, drawled out—'why you must be a thet o' darned fules,--mam and dad's got the eatch a heap wurth than I is, and they thlept in that bed last night when they was here at the quilting.'

The other two strangers were now in a worse predicament than Pete had been, and bouncing from their nest like the house had been on fire, stripped, shook their clothes, put them on again, ordered their horses, and, though it was nearly ten o'clock, they all three left, and rode several miles to the next town before they slept, leaving the imperturbable mail carrier to the bliss of scratching and sleeping alone."[49]

Noland's boisterous Whetstone stories are comic while giving some insight into life in the frontier Arkansas Ozarks. They are rarely outright insulting, using relatively mild dialect and describing the residents of Devil's Fork in an assortment of characteristics that run the gamut from complimentary to the farcical.

*Cover of Noland's book*

Perhaps the most celebrated story of the Ozarks produced by the Southwestern humorists is Thomas Bangs Thorpe's "The Big Bear of Arkansas". Thorpe was definitely an outlander, born, raised and educated in the northeast. But he did spend considerable time in New Orleans and had a love for nature and the outdoors. Published in the *Spirit of the Times* in 1841, Thorpe's tale revolves around backwoodsman and bear hunter Jim Doggett who relates a fantastic hunting story to a diverse group of steamboat passengers on the Mississippi.

Although Doggett is represented as a coarse mountain man, there is something admirable and endearing about the character. Prone to exaggeration, but also self-critical and introspective, Jim Doggett exhibits qualities of native strength and primitive skills. "Big Bear" briefly reveals a depiction of Doggett's home in eastern Arkansas: [50]

"Happen! Happened in Arkansaw: where else could it have happened, but in the creation State, the finishing-up country a State where the sile runs down to the centre of the 'arth, and government gives you a title to every inch of it? Then it airs just breathe them, and they will make you snort like a horse. It's a State without a fault, it is.

Why, stranger, they inhabit the neighborhood of my settlement, one of the prettiest places on old Mississippi, a perfect location, and no mistake; a place that had some defects until the river made the 'cut-off' at 'Shirt-tail bend,' and that remedied the evil, as it brought my cabin on the edge of the river a great advantage in wet weather, I assure you, as you can now roll a barrel of whiskey into my yard in high water from a boat, as easy as falling off a log. It's a great improvement, as toting it by land in a jug, as I used to do, *evaporated* it too fast, and it became expensive.

Just stop with me, stranger, a month or two, or a year, if you like, and you will appreciate my place. I can give you plenty to eat; for beside hog and hominy, you can have bear-ham, and bear sausages, and a mattress of bear-skins to sleep on, and a wild-cat-skin, pulled off hull, stuffed with corn-shucks, for a pillow. That bed would put you to sleep if you had the rheumatics in every joint in your body. I call that ar bed, a *quietus*."

The portrait of Doggett in "Big Bear" is tantalizingly short on his physical characteristics, but provides enough to create an image of the bear hunter:

"There was something about the intruder that won the heart on sight. He appeared to be a man enjoying perfect health and contentment; his eyes were as sparkling as diamonds, and good-natured to simplicity. Then his perfect confidence in himself was irresistibly droll.

When this story was ended, our hero sat some minutes with his auditors, in a grave silence; I saw there was a mystery to him connected with the bear whose death he had just related, that had evidently made a strong impression on his mind. It was also evident that there was some superstitious awe connected with the affair, a feeling common with all "children of the wood," when they meet with anything out of their every-day experience." [51]

Thorpe's Jim Doggett is presented as both admirable and alien, fierce and friendly. Even the dialect Thorpe imposes on Doggett seems fairly realistic and not overly far-fetched. "The Big Bear of Arkansas" is considered an excellent example of Southwestern humor and the tall tale genre in general. It clearly presented an early impression of the Ozarks settler with a combination of strengths and behaviors that could be laudable and distasteful at the same time, particularly to the outlander.

The Big Bear of Arkansas.

*Thomas Bangs Thorpe's illustration from his short story,*
*"The Big Bear of Arkansas"*

Marcus Lafayette Byrn compiled several frontier doctor stories under the pseudonym David Rattlehead in his book *The Life and Adventures of an Arkansaw Doctor*. Born in Tennessee in 1826, he received an M.D. degree from the New York University Medical School and practiced medicine in Tennessee and New York. He was multi-faceted and pursued work as a physician, preacher and hymn composer. Byrn wrote extensively on many topics including medicine, distilling and general knowledge.

Rattlehead's tales may contain some elements of his actual medical practice, but they are so exaggerated and coarse, they fall clearly within the genre of Southwestern humor. Marcus Byrn's time in Arkansas was limited, but his stories, often sold as popular reading material on trains, communicated a rude description of his rural patients to a wide American audience.

Byrn's Rattlehead tales capitalize on the contrast between a so-called sophisticate and the hillfolk. His stories generally seem intended to entertain. Although at times Rattlehead seems to understand the humanity of his patients, he regularly comes across as condescending and even insulting.

In the following excerpt, Byrn manages to insult the terrain, the people and the language of rural Arkansas. It is also another example of comic dialogue between an outlander and a hillbilly.

"One morning while at breakfast, some person hollowed at the gate for me. I went out, and he told me he wanted me to go to see a sick woman some twenty-eight miles across the country. After we got our breakfast we started. We swam our horses across the bayou, and struck a little trail that led through the forest. It was in a different direction from any that I had ever been, and the road was entirely strange to me. I endeavored to notice as many of the peculiarities as possible, knowing I would have to return alone. After passing through many swamps, crossing bayous, cutting cane, and bogging a few times, we arrived safe at the house where the lady was sick. I soon found I had traveled a long ways for little purpose. The patient was an old lady that was of an industrious nature, and the day previous she had been making a big pot of soap which required her attention the whole day. Her husband coming home drunk about dark, had upset the pot, and away went all the woman's hard labor. Returning from the spring with a pail of water on her head, she saw the work of destruction, gave one loud, long, keen 'O, me !' and fell down with a fit of hysterics. This was the first attack she had ever had, and it soon sobered her husband to his senses. In this state of things he ran off for one of his neighbors. All their efforts proved unsuccessful in restoring her to consciousness, and there she lay, gulping and snuffing, without any prospect of relief. They had heard of my whereabouts, and fearing a fatal termination of the case, the old man succeeded in procuring the services of his friend as messenger for me. I found her pretty much as when the messenger started for me.

After resting a few moments, I proceeded to give her a good shower bath; that is, it was not exactly like your city shower baths, water running out of holes made in tin, but pouring a bucketfull or two slap-dash at once. This soon brought her to her natural feelings, and the first thing she said was- 'Tom, you scoundrel, what made you turn over my soap? Now you may wash your own clothes.'

Tom promised to do better in future. This, with two big assa-foetida pills, soon set all right. I gave instructions to the old man how to act should she have another attack; then bidding them good-day, started home. There were but few houses on the way, and I had to travel well to reach the house of an acquaintance about half way between there and home. I thought I could get there by dark. I had gone four or five miles, when I was overtaken by a rain and considerable storm. I sheltered myself under a large bending tree the best I could, and, after the rain was over, started on my way again. I saw it was getting late, six o'clock or later. I made but slow progress, owing to the canes, vines, bushes, &c, being blown across the path. I went on until dark, and as it was yet five miles to the house of my acquaintance, I concluded I had better stop at a little cabin on the road side, just ahead of me. I rode up to the house and hallooed. A little boy out in the woods heard me and came up, when the following dialogue took place.

Doctor.-"My little boy, what's your name? Can I get to stay all night with you?"

Boy.-"Mr. my name is same as my daddy's; don't think you can stay all night here; we no way komidatin' strangers nohow."

Doctor.-"I am willing to put up with any sort of fare, so I can stay; can't you find some place for my horse, and feed him a little?"

Boy.-"Well, I reckin not; for we haint no stable, an' we haint no corn, nor we haint no fodder neder

Doctor.-"Well, if I tie my horse up, can't you find some place for me to sleep?"

Boy.-"Well, I reckin not; kaise we haint no bed, nor we haint no straw, nor we haint no floor in de house nedur."

Doctor.-"That looks pretty bad, my boy; but if I stop, can't you give me something to eat? I feel hungry ; had no dinner to-day."

Boy.-"Well I reckin not; kaise we haint no meet, nur we haint no bred, nor we haint no taiter nedur

Doctor.-"How do you all do about here, then?"

Boy.-"Ah, tolable, thank ye, sir ; how you do yourself? Good-bye, sir-dad's gone out to steal some now." [52]

Albert Pike actually spent considerable time in Arkansas and wrote about his experiences there in realistic and generally favorable terms. Pike was a man of many talents and by today's standards, contradictions. He was a school teacher, a Confederate general, an attorney for Native Americans and a member of the Ku Klux Klan.

In his "Letters from Arkansas" published in *American Monthly Magazine* in 1835, he described a trip he took from Fort Smith down the Arkansas River a short distance. He recounted a small farm he encountered and the homestead's inhabitant. The meeting certainly contains some elements of the Arkansas Traveler story, minus the comic repartee.

*Cover of Byrn's book*

"After travelling over a fine, rolling, upland country, I descended into the bottom of a creek called Little Piney, nine miles from the river — and came at once upon a small log house. I stopped to take a survey before entering; for I had been directed to the settler who lived there. It was like most other settlements in this country. A field of about forty acres was under cultivation, — filled with huge blackened trunks, gigantic skeletons of trees, throwing their bare, withered, sapless branches forth, as though a whirlwind had been among them with its crashing destruction.

About the house were a number of peach trees, scattered about with very little regard to regularity. The house itself was roughly built of logs, and in front was a shelter made of poles, covered with green branches. The owner of the clearing was sitting in front, dressed throughout in leather, and playing lustily on a fiddle. Hearing that sound, I judged there would be no churlishness in his disposition, and I marched boldly up. He greeted me heartily, and without any attempt at politeness, and in two minutes we were on the best terms in the world.

With due reference to those respectable gentlemen of former ages, called troubadours, romancers, et cetera, I incline to believe that the best and most gallant knights of olden time were much such men as the bold and stalwart backwoodsmen. The same bold, brave, and careless demeanor — the same contempt of danger and recklessness of the finer courtesies, and sympathies of life — the same fighting, revelling, carousing, and heedless disposition — the same blunt and unpolished manners exist in the latter which are recorded to have belonged to the former. My present host was one of the purest specimens of the bone and sinew of the West. Tall and athletic, he would hardly have feared a death-grapple with a bear. His frame was close knit, muscular, and well proportioned. He combined the activity of the panther, the strength of the lion, with much of the silent, quick, and stealthy movements of the Indian. He had been a journeyer over deserts and mountains, and a soldier at the battle of New Orleans. Of course he was an excellent Jackson man." [53]

All the Southwestern humorists managed to present a characterization of the Ozarks people that certainly captured some of their strengths while also exaggerating their "otherness". These ongoing depictions in the popular culture of the 19th century would go a long ways toward creating a hillbilly image that was romanticized, but damaging. The comic attributes would stick and last until the present. The class and social distinctions would be permanently etched into the consciousness of the nation, if not the world.

In the second half of the 1800s, a more positive portrait of the Ozarks and its people would begin to emerge. One of these accounts was of the Irish Wilderness.

The mysterious story of the Irish Wilderness experiment provides some insight into the challenges of establishing a successful home or community in the hinterlands of the Ozarks region. Despite good intentions, willing participants and abundant natural resources, carving out a life in the highlands was never easy.

Father John Joseph Hogan was a Catholic priest with a big idea. Born in Ireland in 1829, he immigrated to the United States in 1848, attended seminary in St. Louis and was ordained in 1852. Hogan had a strong desire to perform missionary work, extend Catholic services to regions lacking a priest, and advance the circumstances of the thousands of his fellow Irish immigrating into this country.

In 1857, Father Hogan traveled overland to the wilds of the Ozarks between the Current and Eleven Point Rivers. His goal was to seek land that could be purchased at low prices and homesteaded by poor Irish Americans. He knew that this Ozarks region was not the best for agriculture, but he also knew that with hard work, a living could be extracted from the forests, prairies and bottomland.

With help from the Catholic Church, Hogan either purchased or assisted in the purchase of dozens of parcels of land at prices as low as 12 ½ cents an acre. He helped poor Irish Catholics establish homesteads in the community that would come to be known as the Irish Wilderness.

Little is actually known about conditions at the colony during its short existence. Hogan does give some indication in his memoir *On the Mission in Missouri, 1857-1868* which he published in 1892:

"On a wide and fair tract of ground bought and donated by Reverend James Fox of Old Mines, Missouri, a one story log house forty feet square was erected and partitioned into two apartments, one for a chapel and the other for the priest's residence. Soon improvements went on apace, cutting down trees, splitting rails, burning brushwood, making fences, grubbing roots and stumps, building houses, digging wells, opening roads, breaking and ploughing land, and sowing crops. Already in the spring of 1859, there were about forty families on the newly acquired government lands, or on improved farms purchased, east and west of Current River, in the counties of Ripley and Oregon; and many more were coming, so that the settlement was fairly striding towards final success.

The little chapel amid the forest trees in the wilderness was well attended. Mass, sermon, catechism, confessions, devotions, went on as in old congregations. The quiet solitariness of the place seemed to inspire devotion. Nowhere could the human soul so profoundly worship as in the depths of that leafy forest, beneath the swaying branches of the lofty oaks and pines, where solitude and the heart of man united in praise and wonder of the Great Creator." [54]

For a realist and experienced agrarian, Hogan's description of the bucolic colony he helped found seems rosy and romanticized. It sounds like the Irish community in the wilds was off to a promising start. However, it was not to be.

Hogan left the Irish Wilderness in late 1859 and never returned. He attended to other outreach projects he had started in northwestern Missouri and continued on toward a long life of commitment to the Catholic Church. Though his intentions and hard work for the Irish settlers in the Missouri Ozarks were praiseworthy, he did not foresee the community's collapse under the awful strains of the Civil War.

Already burdened by the difficulties of surviving in the mountain wilds, the conclave was abandoned during the early years of the War Between the States. Assailed by Union troops, Confederate raiders, bushwhackers and violent bandits, the hopeful community dissipated into the old growth pine forest. The Irish Wilderness became a wild place again.

The following brief quote may give some idea as to the Irish settlers' fate:

"An incident as told by Cal Ross, a farmer who lived on Buffalo Creek in Ripley County. 'While threshing wheat with a ground hog thresher near the Hogan Settlement late in the fall of 1863 when Federal Troops scouting the area come on a group of the Irish, opened fire and killed four of the number, and soon after the remainder of the Colony disappeared.'" [55]

It is possible, even likely, that a few Irish colonists remained in the area and resettled following the war. But Hogan's dream of an Irish Catholic conclave along the free flowing rivers was dashed. The area remained a primitive tract, scarcely populated. In the late 1800s and early 1900s, the massive oak, hickory and pine forests were extensively harvested to the point of clearcutting. Not until the mid-twentieth century did the area once again receive attention for its vast beauty and natural features.

Through the establishment of the Mark Twain National Forest in 1939 and the Ozark National Scenic Riverways in 1964, portions of the lands that Father Hogan had once so admired were protected from destruction and overdevelopment. In 1984, over 16,000 acres in Oregon County were dedicated as the Irish Wilderness.

Today, the Current and Eleven Point flow undaunted; the forest, although now almost entirely second-growth, hugs the steep valley walls and rocky ridges; the glades and mountain meadows open up with windblown wildflowers. Deer, turkey and the occasional bear haunt the hills and hollows. No one lives here now; it is a wilderness. There are really no signs of Father Hogan's dream; perhaps some loose stones or a depression in the ground. The hardy souls who tried to make a life here couldn't overcome the winds of war and the harsh requirements of primitive Ozark existence. [56]

The Civil War laid waste to much of the Ozarks. Arkansas was admitted to the Union in 1836 as a slave state and seceded to join the Confederacy in 1861. Missouri received statehood in 1821, also as a slave state. Arkansas fought and lost the Civil War as part of the rebel army. Missouri was a mess.

Missouri was a border and frontier state that contained all the elements of the protracted ideologies and disputes over the slavery issue. With strong Southern sympathies, the state government was initially pro-Confederacy and sought to secede. Despite some early Confederate success, pro-North elements won out and Missouri remained in the Union. A Missouri Confederate government-in-exile existed during the remainder of the war, but essentially had no state power.

Missouri saw many battles throughout the Civil War and played an important role in control of the Mississippi and Missouri River corridors. In the Ozarks region of southern Missouri bordering Arkansas, major and minor conflicts erupted throughout the hill country and surrounding region.

Arkansas also played a key role in the Civil War's western campaigns, particularly in control of the Arkansas and Mississippi Rivers. Following the Battle of Pea Ridge in early 1862, Union occupancy of northwest Arkansas led to considerable depopulation and destruction of one of the more developed regions in the state.[57]

In addition to engagements between the two armies, violence proliferated in the Ozarks. Acts of atrocity were committed by both sides with civilians often on the receiving end. Bands of semi-military vigilantes and outright criminals took advantage of the chaos and plagued the hill country. People were murdered, their crops and livestock stolen, their homes burned, and their livelihoods destroyed.

In a region where existence was already demanding, the Civil War made life almost impossible. Many families were forced to abandon their homesteads. The Ozarks, an area already sparsely populated, became even more empty and desolate.

Sila Turnbo's manuscripts include multiple stories of the hardships and savagery of the Civil War era. The following tale describes both the awful conditions of life in the border region and the animosity created by the disorder: [58]

"The writer received the following history of an incident that occurred in the bloody days of the Civil War. This was written at Arlington, Washington, by J. D. Row under date of August 11, 1907. Mr. Row wrote that he learned it from an old timer who lived on Bee Creek which has its source in North Boone County, Arkansas, and empties into White River in Taney County, Missouri. Here is the way he told it to me.

When the war come up the people who lived in what is now Boone County, Arkansas, were divided in their political views. Many honest souls went into the southern service, others went with the north. Several of the men in the federal army were located at Springfield, Missouri, and their families were having a seriously hard time at their homes. Some of their neighbors who sympathized with the south were not manly enough to go into the regular service and they took pleasure in making it as disagreeable for these women and their children as they could. Finally three of these families decided to yoke up a span of oxen to each of their wagons and make their way to Springfield where their husbands were located, in the northern army. They had but fairly got started when they were overtaken by several of their reckless neighbors, boys and men. They were set out of their wagons by the road-side, their wagons and contents set on fire, and their oxen driven away. They were more than 60 miles from Springfield without food and shelter and nothing but their scanty clothes on their backs, nothing at home to go back to. They wended their way on foot toward their destination. In 12 days of destitution and untold suffering they reached their husbands and fathers in Springfield. One sweet little child was laid away in the cold ground by the way side. The whole union force was much exasperated at such treatment given to help-less women and children. Their starved and almost naked condition corroborated the account of their ill treatment. The officers in command told the men whose families had been treated so cruelly, to pick out what help they thought they needed, from the command, and go and teach that neighborhood a lasting lesson. About 25 men took the Fort Smith road which lead them into Carroll County. From there they went east into what is now the middle of Boone County. The women had given the names of their assailants, and they knew where to find where they lived. From about the vicinity of where Harrison on Crooked Creek now is these twenty-five men went north and visited the homes of each person who had taken part in abusing these women. They would call at the yardgate and woe to the man, or boy of any site, who appeared at the door. They would throw leaden balls till their victims sank down, then ride on in haste to the next man's house who had been named by the women. Among the band that had done the awful deed was one young man by the name of Denton. The women had not stated to their husbands and friends that it was the young Denton and when the soldiers called at the Denton house the old gentleman opened the door fearlessly, and as he stood in the midst of the open door he received the first ball that was fired at him which took effect in his bowels. He immediately sank to the floor and the men silently rode away. But he did not die. He recovered and lived until about the year 1898 when he died. When the war come up he told his two or three boys who were nearly grown that they must remain at home if it was possible to do so, attend to their own business, and let all others do what they may. But when the war spirit took possession of them they got into many desperate affairs and difficulties. Mr. Denton said afterward that he had to suffer for the meanness of his boys."

Turnbo's explicit stories shine a harsh light on life in the Ozarks during and after the Civil War. People had fled their homes, some to never return. The way of life for the mountain folk had been severely interrupted. Their isolation and independence had been challenged and altered. As Rebecca Howard says in her doctoral dissertation on the Civil War period in northwest Arkansas: [59]

"The civilian experience in northwest Arkansas, however, laid the foundation for postwar life in the area. By the end of the war, the civilian population was focused on survival, and Union or Confederate affiliation mattered much less than it had at the beginning of the war as civilians faced the undisciplined violence that had taken over the region. Even Robert Mecklin, who early in his correspondence was careful to identify the affiliation of every villain in the area, by 1864 increasingly labels all as 'robbers.' The post colonies protected any civilian ready to swear loyalty to the Union, no matter their previous affiliation, but this common cause during desperate times would be challenged as the war ended and Confederates returned, even though unionists kept the upper hand in both northwest Arkansas, and the state government."

Following the battles at Pea Ridge and Prairie Grove, Union forces occupied northwest Arkansas and moved east to consolidate their hold on the region. Although there were few major battles between the two armies, guerilla warfare raged across the northern tier of Arkansas. Bands of guerillas, some sanctioned by the Confederacy and some extra-military, continually harassed the Federal troops, Union sympathizers, and in some cases, what remained of the general population.

The war's impact on the Arkansas Ozarks was devastating. The hard scrabble existence of the mountain folk was exacerbated by confiscation of their provisions, widespread destruction of property, and even outright murder by both sides.

Daniel E. Sutherland describes this period in his essay, "Guerillas: The Real War in Arkansas": [60]

"Revenge and personal vendetta also counted for much. The origins of this impulse varied. Some people sought revenge against neighbors who had persecuted them for supporting the 'wrong' side. Others used the war as an excuse to right old wrongs and settle family feuds. Revenge also explains why partisans, as well as men in the regular forces, sometimes crossed the line between soldier and brigand. Once violence had been done to one's family, neighbors, or home, retaliation frequently followed."

The Civil War would have a lasting impact on the way Americans viewed their neighbors. From a very broad view, for some in the North, Southerners had confirmed their image as a backward, prejudiced people. Similarly, for some in the South, Northerners were seen as condescending, exploitive interlopers.

At a narrow, but very personal level, the experiences of individual Union soldiers during the war added to the perceptions that much of the country would accept about the South and specifically about the Ozarks. As the Union army invaded and occupied northern Arkansas, the experiences of the troops, mostly from the northern plains States, would create an indelible image of the land and people of the Ozarks region.

William L. Shea researched and compiled the personal letters and writings of individual Union soldiers who were part of the North's campaign into northern Arkansas. His research reveals common impressions of the region. [61]

"What shortly before had been considered a mountainous wonderland now was described as a 'gloomy and forbidding region of chert hills and pine forests,' 'a country of the most weird and uninviting character,' 'an uninhabited, cheerless, and arid region,' and 'the most desolate country I ever saw,' crisscrossed by the 'awfulest roads man ever traveled.'"

And perhaps even more damaging were the impressions these young men took home of the hill country's inhabitants:

"Quite a number of soldiers remarked that the natives—later generations would derisively call them hillbillies—matched their ramshackle buildings. One man observed that 'there is a general appearance of slovenliness, as if they had all come to the conclusion that there was no use trying to be decent.'" [62]

The opinions that these combatants formed were surely colored by the tribulations of war and their alienation in an unfamiliar land. Nevertheless, they carried these feelings home and surely spread them to their family and friends. Their impressions did not have the widespread dissemination of the media or the popular writings of the day. But they were powerful in the fact that they were personal and ingrained as first-hand experience. Fair or not, the soldiers' beliefs about the Ozarks and its people were permanently impressed on some.

One trait often associated with the negative hillbilly image is that of a people prone to feuding. This perception may have its roots in the stories formulated by chroniclers and outlander writers who emphasized what they saw as the violent tendencies of mountain people. In actuality, the Ozarks folk are probably no more prone to feuding than any other regional group, particularly in a frontier setting. The stigma of feuding has most likely been assigned to Ozarkians due to sensationalized media coverage of conflicts between groups already represented as "primitive" and "others". The Civil War only exacerbated these impressions.

The following story of the Williams family of Conway County, Arkansas as told by Kenneth C. Barnes highlights the human emotions that were aggravated by the War Between the States. [63]

Conway County, straddling the Arkansas River in the southern Ozarks, was home to the Williams family, Unionists in a Confederate State. Jeff Williams, his four brothers, three sisters, and their families homesteaded in Conway and Van Buren Counties in 1844. Jeff Williams was a successful farmer, preacher and owner of one slave.

The Williams were staunchly opposed to secessionism and publicly expressed their views. They were apparently not opposed to slavery, but along with many other Arkansans were against their State leaving the Union. Following secession, Unionists across northern Arkansas formed "Peace Societies" with the intended purpose of protecting their property and families from Confederate retribution.

Some Arkansas Unionists tried to lay low and avoid confrontations and conscription into the Confederate army, some joined guerilla bands to defend their own and harass the opposition, and some actually joined the Union army. In 1862, Jeff Williams and several of his male family members enlisted with the North. They hoped they would be used as the basis for a local militia to guard their home territory, but they would be disappointed.

Mustered in at Batesville, the Williams and other Arkansas Unionists ended up marching south along the White River to Helena. Here the Union force languished. Disease was rampant. Serving as part of the First Arkansas Infantry Battalion, the Williams clan saw only one actual battle and spent the rest of their six months service scrounging for provisions and fighting disease. Nearly half of Jeff Williams' infantry company of seventy-five men died from disease; none died in battle.

Eventually, what remained of the Williams men relocated to Springfield, Missouri where they were able to relocate some of their family members who had been stranded in Arkansas. After Union forces consolidated their hold on northern Arkansas in 1863, Jeff Williams was finally able to return to his home in Conway County. Here they formed what they had always hoped for — a local militia. Jeff Williams was made commander of the company which included many of his surviving family members.

With the Union army controlling north Arkansas, guerilla warfare proliferated throughout the region. The Williams clan provided support for the Union effort and attempted to protect their own interests. They repeatedly clashed with local rebel bands. In 1865, Jeff Williams was killed by Confederate guerillas led by Colonel Witt. Jeff's son Leroy and other family members pursued the rebels and killed several of them. Leroy Williams' exploits would become Arkansas legend.

During Reconstruction, violence continued in Conway County just as it did across the entire Ozarks. Old antipathies led to feuds and acts of revenge. Elements of personal, political and racial conflict inflamed by the Civil War plagued the region for years. Into the twentieth century, fierce social and political battles resulted in lynchings, assassination, voter fraud and Jim Crow politics.

"Doubtless, the story of the Williams clan is like that of many ordinary mountain folk of the state. For the Williams family and their neighbors of Conway County, the war meant disruption of their family life, tragic violence which took life on both sides of the conflict, and a cycle of retributive feuding which continued for generations." [64]

When the war ended, settlers slowly returned to their mountain cabins and farms. They had to rekindle old relationships and form new ones. They had to start over with the determination and toil they had relied on before. The war may have been over, but animosity and old feuds remained. The Ozark Mountains would continue to be a region pocked with violence. This image would carry on the perception of hillbilly brutishness and lawlessness some of the chroniclers of the hill country had described during the previous half century.

Reconstruction attempted to forcefully integrate the secessionists back into the Union fold. The states were formally united again, but people and their political and social beliefs were another matter. Long-held animosity and mistrust were only exaggerated by the war, vigilantism, general lawlessness, and forced compliance. Black people were freed on paper, but achieving parity would be an ongoing battle, continuing to the present. The Reconstruction era would result in swift and chronic actions by some to thwart emancipation and the strength of Republican policies.

At the same time that political power was seized by the Republicans and resisted by the Democrats, other social, economic and cultural changes were occurring throughout the Ozarks. As populations began to rebound and new immigrants (often from northern states) entered the region, towns began to grow. A new dynamic between town elites and rural dwellers entered the scene.

The elites, the businessmen, politicians, professional people, and large land owners strove to improve economic conditions. But often, they promoted their own advancement at the expense of the rural poor and the small farmer. "Carpetbaggers" and "Scalawags" may have declared their intent to bring order and prosperity to the war-ravaged area of southern Missouri and northern Arkansas, but they also brought elements of injustice, graft and classism.

Faced with trying to improve the area's image and well-being, the elites would intentionally or not, create a division between the haves and have-nots of the Ozarks. Now the hillbilly was not just an "other" in the eyes of outlanders; he was considered a hindrance to the advancement of modernity within the hill country.

Towns grew, railroads began to enter the Ozarks and commerce began to improve in the region. But at the same time, vigilantism and poverty continued to plague the interior mountain regions.

The upland regions of the Ozarks, including the Boston Mountains, the St. Francois Mountains, and the White River Hills are dotted with high, rounded rises called knobs. Before deforestation, many of these hills were bare on their peaks, sometimes with a single, lone pine dubbed a signal tree. The bald knobs were excellent outlooks to view the surrounding countryside and served as easily identified meeting places. In the late 1800s, these hills gave their name to the Bald Knobbers.

The Bald Knobbers were first organized in Taney County, Missouri as The League for Law and Order in 1885. The group was formed to combat local lawlessness. The League was originally composed of about a dozen members, including ex-Union soldiers, business owners, a minister, and two attorneys.

The League sought out and punished those who they felt had committed criminal acts. The lynching of the Taylor brothers, who were being held in the Forsyth jail after admitting to their involvement in the shooting of a store owner and his wife, was attributed to the League. This incident led to the formation of an anti-Bald Knobber group.

Acts of vigilantism and revenge occurred for several months between the two rival bands. Their deeds received attention across the state. In April, 1886, the Bald Knobbers officially disbanded after about fifteen months of operation. But unofficially, groups of vigilantes and para-military gangs continued to operate and spread their violence to neighboring counties. In the name of "law and order", individuals and organized groups took it upon themselves to enact their own form of justice, carry out vengeance on their opponents and enemies, and extract personal and political gain. These incidents and events would result in feuds and resentments that would last for decades, continuing the harsh animosity resulting from the Civil War. [65]

In 1886, Nathan Kinney, a leader of the original Bald Knobbers, shot and killed Andrew Coggburn at the old Oak Grove Schoolhouse east of Branson. The killing was supposedly a duel for "honor", but certainly carried the earmarks of vigilantism. Kinney himself was shot and killed by Billy Miles two years later as an act of revenge. [66]

In his article "Where Did All the Money Go" local historian Lynn Morrow gives a comprehensive examination of how local economics impacted the lawlessness in the southern border counties of Missouri, specifically Taney County, following the Civil War.

Morrow places some of the blame for the "Border War" on vacillating political turmoil and fiscal corruption within county government. In evaluating the poor fiscal condition of Taney County in the years following the war, Morrow details the mismanagement of public monies and then asks, "Whatever the fiscal circumstances were, Taney County presiding justices and their clerks in the 1870s and early 1880s never satisfactorily answered the fundamental question -- Where did all the money go?" [67]

The Bald Knobber saga and the economic debacle in Taney County, Missouri are examples of the difficulties experienced across the Ozarks region. Although certainly not confined to the Ozarks, the upheavals of the Reconstruction era added to the perception that rural people and particularly the hillfolk were prone to backwardness, feuding and lawlessness.

*Still shot from the movie "Baldknobber" released in 2017*

Nearly every culture has its alcoholic beverage. The imbibing of ethanol is as ubiquitous as laughing and language. For some, when one thinks of the hillbilly, the images of moonshine immediately come to mind. The production, selling and consumption of white lightning has become intertwined with the perceptions of mountain life.

Hillfolk have no monopoly on liquor making or its use. But something about the bucolic image of hidden stills, Mason jars and running from the revenuers seems to have stuck to the hillbilly persona. Perhaps the perceptions of rural distilling started with the Whiskey Rebellion of 1791.

After institution of a federal tax on distilled spirits, frontier residents of western Pennsylvania protested, declaring the levy unfair and a violation of their rights. They refused to pay the tax and resisted through several violent confrontations. Eventually, President George Washington led a large militia force to Pennsylvania and the rebellion was resolved without additional violence.

But the production of illegal booze did not end. Many boot-leggers merely moved their operation to hidden locales and sold their wares clandestinely. Particularly in rural areas, the production of spirits from excess grain crops was a useful means for generating cash income. Using recipes handed down from generations of distillers and home-made stills, the making of moonshine was an accepted craft, particularly in the hills of the Appalachian Mountains.

Since 1791, excise taxes on alcohol have come and gone, but since the early 1900s, all states and the Federal government have imposed these levies to varying degrees. The most stringent restriction on liquor came during Prohibition which prohibited the production, importation, transportation and sale of alcoholic beverages from 1920 to 1933.

Although initially widely supported politically and generally considered to have had some positive impacts on health, Prohibition could not contain people's thirst for ethanol. Belief that the law was responsible for increases in organized crime, reduction in tax revenue, and a negative impact on agriculture led to repeal of the law by the Twenty-first Amendment.

The association of moonshine stills with mountain people is probably a result of their prejudicial portrayal as backwards, shiftless and unlawful. In reality, the making and use of liquor is probably no more common among rural folks than it is urban dwellers. In fact, alcohol consumption is usually lower in rural areas compared to urban settings. Beginning in the late nineteenth century and gathering steam in the early 1900s, opposition to alcohol was strong in the Ozarks. [68]

Bootlegging seems to have a certain aura of craftiness and independence that may fit well with some hillbilly portrayals, but one must also consider the economic practicalities of moonshining. Subsistence farming produces little cash income. Using small quantities of grain for distilling is a smart way to generate a product for personal use and make some sorely needed cash money.

Moonshine was not an uncommon commodity in the Ozarks, but its manufacture and use has probably been overblown by fictional accounts and pandering anecdotes. In the mountains, illicit distilling could often be associated with economic conditions and conflict between poor farmers and local law enforcement.

*Still in Pineville 1931*

In the 1890s, the Harve Bruce family was struggling to withstand an economic depression that had gripped the entire country. Faced with possible foreclosure on his rugged 160-acre homestead in Van Buren County, Arkansas, Bruce became a moonshiner.

Spurred on by local prohibitionists, federal and local officers made a raid on Harve Bruce's home in 1897. A confrontation resulted and although Bruce was not apprehended, he did move a part of his operation to nearby Pope County. A few days later, Federal Marshalls Benjamin Taylor and Joe Dodson along with several local posse members raided Bruce's new still. In the ensuing shootout, both Taylor and Dodson were killed and two others were injured. Harve Bruce was wounded, but escaped and fled the area.

The killing of two federal agents and the unseemly activities surrounding this affair created a spate of sensational news reporting throughout the region. The *New York Times* published several stories about the event which contributed to a perception of illegal and violent behavior infesting the Ozarks. Federal and local law enforcement was stepped up considerably resulting in the destruction of several stills and the arrest of many local illicit distillers. Fear and mistrust reigned throughout the local populace.

Over the next several months Harve Bruce and some of his compatriots were captured, tried and convicted of illegal production of alcohol and sentenced to prison terms at Fort Leavenworth. In 1899, Bruce was tried for murder in Pope County. He claimed he was the only one that had shot at the marshals during the raid and that he did so in self-defense after they fired first.

Bruce was convicted of involuntary manslaughter and sentenced to six months in the state prison, but was eventually pardoned by populist Governor Jeff Davis. Harve Bruce's reputation was forever judged by the perspective of the viewer: the poor Ozark farmer, the local town elite, the prohibitionist, the national reading public. [69]

"Bruce's own explanation [for why he made moonshine], however, pointed to practical economic necessities in the rural Ozarks rather than some anti-government hill culture and knee-jerk reaction against authorities telling him what he could and could not do. When asked by the Conway newspaper reporter why he and his Ozarks neighbors flaunted the federal and state laws against making moonshine, 'Bruce explained that their corn was worth only 30 cents per bushel. When they made it into whiskey the slop was worth as much as the corn to feed the hogs and they could get $2.00 per gallon for the whiskey. This was the only way, he explained, of getting any money up there in the mountains.'" [70]

While hunting, Nathan Lilly leaned his shotgun against a fence. As he climbed over the wire, the weapon fell, discharged and tore into his right arm just below the shoulder. Nathan was rushed to the local physician who amputated his arm with a hacksaw.

It was hard enough to eke out a living on their Christian County, Missouri farm along Bull Creek during the Great Depression. Now Nathan had only one arm. Struggling to support his young family, he turned to moonshining. In 1938, Lilly was arrested for illegal spirit making and sent to prison, leaving his pregnant wife Mary Lou alone.

On a cold spring day, Mary Lou, unassisted, alone and frightened gave birth to a son. Little Georgie only survived twelve hours. Despondent, the young mother bathed the child, wrapped him in a blanket, and carried him to the cemetery. She found an obelisk-shaped creek stone and carved Georgie's initial into the soft limestone marker.

Released from prison, Nathan Lilly returned home and with Mary Lou, raised a family on the ridge above Bull Creek. Nathan found work with the WPA and later travelled to the West Coast for work during World War II. Despite hardships, the Lillys found a way to survive and thrive.

Over the years, Mary Lou often walked to the cemetery and placed flowers on the grave of little George, the first-born she had lost. His gravestone was replaced with a more conventional marker. The peaceful spot along the banks of Bull Creek became a melancholy, but somehow heartening reminder of loss, struggle, forbearance and triumph. [71]

The hills of the Ozarks can be beautiful, but demanding. They can knock you down and pick you up. They can give and provide and then snatch away hard-earned victories. The people of the Ozarks, the mountaineers, the hillbillies have had to adapt and learn the lessons of their challenging environment. Some succeed, some do not. Regardless of the criticism, the condescension, the mocking and the categorizing, the people of the Ozarks uplift must be recognized for their hardiness, their adaptable spirit and their ingenuity in creating a culture that is unique, creative and worthy.

Following the Civil War, Ozark hillbillies worked to reestablish their livelihoods and mountain way of life as new forces began to enter the region. Transportation had always been difficult in the Ozarks, but improvements were coming. In the late

1800s, railroads began snaking tentacles from the perimeter into the rough terrain of the interior mountains.

In 1858, the St. Louis, Iron Mountain and Southern Railway reached Pilot Knob extending service into the iron ore and timber areas of the southeastern Ozarks. In 1881, the Frisco extended from Monett, Missouri to Fayetteville, Arkansas. The Missouri and North Arkansas Railroad reached Eureka Springs in 1883. It was not until 1906 that the White River Line of the Missouri Pacific Railroad completed its tortuous route through the White River Hills from Carthage, through Aurora, Reeds Spring and Branson and on to Newport, Arkansas.

These mountain railroads required heavy capital investment and were very difficult to build. The interior lines had to cross rivers and streams on bridges, tunnel through the mountains, and span wide valleys on high wooden trestles.

The railroads were a boost to the regional economy and provided access to outside markets. They brought manufactured goods into the hill country and were a connection between the Ozarks and a broader America. Building the railroads provided work for many local people.

The hardwood and pine forests of the White River Valley were heavily logged in the late 1800s and early 1900s. As the railroads pushed west and through the Ozarks, there was a huge demand for lumber, particularly for railroad ties. Large tracts were clearcut throughout southern Missouri and northern Arkansas. Between 1910 and 1925, Reeds Spring was the largest supplier of white oak railroad ties in the United States. Often, cut timber was floated down streams in tie rafts. When pines and hardwoods were removed from the forests and savannahs, cedars often became the dominant tree. Eventually, even cedars were widely harvested for furniture, fence posts and pencils.

Tie hacking was practiced by many local residents as a source of revenue. This was difficult and dangerous work, but helped many families earn extra cash income. Oak was the most desired tree for ties and oak was abundant on the verdant hills of the White River.

Prior to European settlement, seventy percent of Missouri was forested, including over six million acres of shortleaf pine.

Most of the pine was growing in the Courtois Hills region of southeastern Missouri, but pine groves existed across the southern tier of the state and throughout Arkansas. Pine was a valuable resource for the expanding population of the Ozarks in the late 1800s. Supported by the railroads and capital investments by eastern and mid-western industrialists, largescale sawmills were established across the Ozarks.

One of the largest mills was the Missouri Lumber and Mining Company at Grandin in Carter County. From 1887 to 1909, the Grandin Mill clearcut up to seventy acres a day of virgin Ozark pine forest. Throughout the region, sawmills snaked their narrow gauge railways into the forests and removed the trees. The lumber furnished a needed resource for a growing nation and provided employment for many local hillfolk.

But eventually the pines and much of the hardwood were extracted with no plans for reforestation. The mills closed, the jobs disappeared and the stricken land was abandoned. The inhabitants of the hill country were left with eroded soil, gravel-filled streams, and a severe reduction in wildlife. These impacts only exacerbated the mountain folks' lifestyle.

Eventually, through the establishment of state conservation departments and the creation of the Mark Twain and Ozark National Forests, much of the Ozarks region was reforested and managed under modern forestry practices. But it has been difficult to reestablish the shortleaf pine. Today there are stands of pine in the Missouri and Arkansas Ozarks, but they are nothing like the old growth forest that once existed. [72]

In 1951, Leo Drey purchased a large acreage in Shannon County. Drey had a dream to establish an extensive forest area that could be managed for sustained growth while protecting the environmental uniqueness and identity of the Ozarks. His dream became a reality as the Pioneer Forest and would grow to encompass 150,000 acres.

For seventy years, the Pioneer Forest has represented methods of single-tree forestry management and the conservation of wildlife, water resources and Ozark biosystems that protect and sustain both the environment and the region's economy.

In 2004, Drey and his wife Kay donated their ownership of the Pioneer lands to the L-A-D Foundation (for Leo A. Drey). This gift, valued at $180 million, was one of the largest philanthropic donations in the country that year. Drey's significant commitment and investment in the Pioneer Forest reflects his interest in recognizing and sustaining the environmental and cultural aspects of the Ozark Mountains. [73]

*(left to right): Ed Woods, Leo Drey, and Charlie Kirk*
*L-A-D Foundation*

Perhaps the greatest social impact the railroads had on the Ozarks was the nexus created between outlanders (tourists) and local inhabitants. The initial draw was for the hunting and fishing opportunities the area held. Wealthy people from mid-western cities particularly were attracted to the hills for outdoor sports. And the railways provided a quick and reasonably comfortable means to connect.

Once in the area, these sportsmen required guides. And the local hillbillies knew where and how to find game and fish. The mountainmen had relied on hunting and fishing for their sustenance. Now they realized they could also trade these skills for cash.

There must have been a mutual arrangement between these disparate associates — the city fellow relying on the local for information, assistance and a successful outing; the guide relying on the outlander for cooperation and payment. Both players were interacting with someone with little commonality, other than a love for the outdoors.

There are few reports of negative experiences between the tourists and the guides. The visitors knew they were relying on locals who had been reported (at least in popular media) to be obstinate, ignorant, and even violent. The guides knew they were working with clients who probably looked down on them and would likely try to cheat them.

So how did these business arrangements work out? There must have been some sort of respect and cooperation that developed. What was said out of earshot by either side would probably reveal common misjudgments and prejudices. But on the water or in the woods, there had to be accepted trust and cooperation.

Just as in the writings of the outlanders who visited the Ozarks in the early 1800s, there were elements of respect and recognition that the hillbillies certainly had positive characteristics. The float trips and hunting expeditions that developed in the late nineteenth century would grow into an expansive tourist business in the Ozarks.

The image of the hillbilly would continue to take on dual elements of admiration and derision. People would flock to the Ozarks to see a "real hillbilly". The tourists' impressions of the mountaineers would not converge with the reality. In mass media, the exploitation of the hillbilly image would continue to be either comic or derisive. But yet the vacationers came. Some came and did not understand. Some came and realized there was truly an alternate image. Some came and stayed, understanding that the lifeways of the hillfolk, although different than their own, was an existence both admirable and honorable.

# Chapter 3

## Hillfolk and Hillbillies

*Charlie Barnes* was one of the great river men of the Ozarks. He designed and built hundreds of craft that would come to be known as johnboats. Charlie called them "float boats". Born in 1878, Charlie spent his life on the James River in Galena and later in Branson on the White.

Charlie was a man of many talents. He loved spending time on the river fishing, floating and guiding big city clients. In 1904, Charlie and his brothers Herb and John started the Barnes Brothers Boating Company out of Galena. They would guide their customers down the James and White, sometimes as far as Cotter, Arkansas. In those days, the rivers ran free. Floats could last up to two weeks or longer.

The Barnes brothers outfitted their float boats to take sportsmen and sportswomen down the Ozarks streams, put them on fish and set up camps on the gravel bars, sheltered under the massive cottonwoods and beneath the big, blue Ozarks sky.

Charlie modified early river boats to better meet the needs of his float business. His wood of choice was pine. Wider and not as long as the "gigging" boats, Charlie's float boats had some upward rake at the bow and stern. Guides like Barnes could make these craft dance on the water, shooting the rapids, holding near the fishy pools, and skimming lightly down the long river stretches. These watercraft were stable and could carry the heavy load of supplies required for a multiple-day trip down the river.

The float fishing clients came mostly from the big mid-western cities: Springfield, St. Louis, Kansas City, even Chicago. Over its years in business, the Barnes Brothers Boating Company entertained celebrities like Gene Autry, Forrest Tucker, Tennessee Ernie Ford, Smiley Burnette and nationally known sports writer Robert Page Lincoln. Charlie welcomed these wealthy sportsmen to his environment.

The relationship between Charlie Barnes and his float customers must have been one of mutual respect and trust. These clients would not have come or returned to visit the hill country if they did not have confidence in their guides and their skills. In an article in the Missouri Conservationist, Charlie's son Bill gives some insight into his father's personality: [74]

"Of the hundreds of people who Charlie Barnes took down the Ozark rivers, one suspects that some were not fun to be with, but Bill Barnes says that his dad knew how to handle them. 'He was not a man of many words,' Bill says. 'If he had complaints you didn't know it ... very likely he said nothing.'"

In addition to running his float fishing business, Charlie was fascinated by the "horseless carriage". Around 1915, Charlie bought a Ford Model T. The Barnes brothers opened a Ford dealership on the square in Galena, but they never lost their love of being on the water. Bill Barnes says, "Sometimes we'd close the garage for the afternoon and make a half day float back down to Galena. Other times we would wait until the end of the day and we would go out camping and trotlining at night." [75]

Charlie also worked for Jim Owen's float trip business in Branson. He built boats for Owen and arranged guides for excursions on the Current, Jacks Fork, Kings and Buffalo Rivers. He left a rich heritage of floating the streams of the Ozarks and introducing outlanders to the beauty and hospitality of the mountain waterways. A Kansas City Star article in later years said, "The 78 year-old Barnes had a special hankering ... since the age of eight he has probably spent more time than anyone else on the White and James rivers with float fishing his main purpose. As for the johnboat he's no doubt the world's number one authority; all he did was introduce it to the Ozarks some 58 years ago." [76]

So did Charlie Barnes' float fishing clients think he was a hillbilly? Perhaps. Did they consider him in a pejorative sense? Probably not. Outlanders and rural elites alike frequently interacted with people like Charlie Barnes. These interactions were mostly positive and must have contributed to a complementary view of the hillfolk. Perhaps these constructive opinions were limited to short-lived contacts or existed as romanticized beliefs.

***Charlie Barnes***

Phyllis Rossiter, in her comprehensive book *A Living History of the Ozarks*, comments on the relationship between the river guides and their clients: [77]

"Partially because of the 'mystique' of these river-wise and outgoing natives with peppery personalities — and the charm endowed to 'hillbilly' culture in general by the outsiders — the guides themselves often became local celebrities. Customers often returned just to further enjoy the guide's company and told others who came seeking a similar experience. Indeed, floaters frequently chose their guides as much for their ability to tell colorful stories and jokes as for their prowess with a johnboat; that was a given."

The Chamberlain family operated Camp Rock Haven on the James River at Cape Fair from the 1930s until Table Rock Lake flooded the resort forever in 1958. As a young man, Scotty Chamberlin worked hard every day at his family's resort and interacted with the clients who came to enjoy the float fishing experience. As a boy he didn't guide much, but was responsible for much of the equipment associated with the float service.

Scotty organized all the gear necessary for a day's float. The commissary included boats, chairs and paddles, food, ice chests, cooking utensils, tents, cots and bedding. Scotty helped gather the gear, load the johnboats and transport the float clients to their put-in site. As a youth, Scotty would shuttle anglers to and from the river in a 1½ ton Chevy long-bed truck. The vehicle was a converted Coca-Cola truck with dual rear tires. Scotty learned early to navigate the rough river roads. The roads were not much more than trails, cleared down to ledgerock and graveled, often just one lane. Punctures were frequent on the flint strewn roads and Scotty became efficient at repairing flats on the rayon tires.

In the evening, many float anglers would return from the river to Camp Rock Haven. They would eat supper at the Rock Haven Cafe (later the Fisherman's Hat Cafe) operated by Scotty's mother Alma, with the assistance of some of the float guides' wives. During the winter, the Chamberlains would hold lively square dances at the camp.

Scotty Chamberlin relates the story behind the Fisherman's Hat Cafe's name:

"The customers would leave their favorite fishing hats with their favorite fishing lures on the walls of the cafe. When returning, they would don their hats and declare their desire to 'hit the river'. The cafe was the local hangout for the guides in hopes of picking up a stray guide job."

Scotty's work continued with cleaning, sorting and restocking the equipment for the next day's float. Laundry at the camp was cleaned in an old wringer washer, hung out to dry and pressed in an "Ironrite". For several years, the only electricity at Camp Rock Haven was supplied by a Delco gasoline-powered generator. The generator charged a bank of batteries which powered lights, refrigerators, pumps and equipment. Ozark Electric ran power to the area after World War II. The original well at Camp Rock Haven was a hand-dug well. Later, a mechanically drilled well was bored on the property.

Rock Haven was the first location to have telephone service on the lower James. Scotty's father Lyle Chamberlain had an early mobile phone in his 1932 Ford. The wireless system connected to Marionville and then Springfield.

Camp Rock Haven was located on the river bottomland near the end of the original Cape Fair Bridge. The river often flooded, not only covering the bridge, but causing damage to the camp. After a flood, the Chamberlains had to thoroughly clean and repair the cabins. On one occasion, the high water moved one cabin completely off its foundation.

Scotty Chamberlin says of his life at Camp Rock Haven:

"I didn't know anything else. I just thought everybody else had that, where you worked day and night. The minute you got up in the morning, like six o'clock in the morning, you were busy until midnight. I thought everybody lived that way." [78]

*Camp Rock Haven on the James River*

Scotty's time on the Ozarks float stream reveals a life of hard work, close interaction with nature, and cooperation between residents of the hills and the float fishing clients who came mostly from the larger towns and cities of the mid-West. The float camps relied on their customers who provided their source of income. And the vacationers relied on the camp operators and the guides for safe and enjoyable excursions. These relationships had to be based on mutual respect and communication. These folk may have come from different worlds, but they came together and communed in a still rugged and wild environment.

*Lyle Chamberlain and a float client*

Whatever their duration or endurance, the view of the hillbilly personae had begun to change by the turn of the century. There were elements of the often begrudging admiration shown by some of the nineteenth century chroniclers and even the Southwestern humorists. There were comic and offensive characterizations that would continue and grow in mainstream media. But one of the tracks the hillbilly image would take, at least as viewed by many outlanders, was the notion of a natural, nostalgic personality, living close to nature with honest, traditional skills. This view was encouraged by the growing popularity of the Arcadian movement and reaction against the evils of urbanization and industrialization.

The float fishing business was one of the drivers behind interest in the Ozarks. Other forces at work were the back to the land movement and a renewed interest in rural living. Romanticized stories of pastoral life and the benefits of clean water, clean air and rejuvenating springs would gain national attention by the early twentieth century.

Harold Bell Wright's *The Shepherd of the Hills* is the best example of a turn-of-the-century romanticized novel about the Ozarks. Wright, a minister, made several trips to the White River country between 1896 and 1904. His sojourns were intended to improve his health, but he fell in love with the area and its people and it provided considerable inspiration for his writing. In 1907, he published his novel about life in the White River Hills near the Notch post office.

*The Shepherd of the Hills* contains exuberant depictions of the hillfolk characters as seen in Wright's representation of the novel's ingenue Sammy Lane: [79]

"Miss Sammy Lane was one of those rare young women whose appearance is not to be described. One can, of course, put it down that she was tall; beautifully tall, with the trimness of a young pine, deep bosomed, with limbs full-rounded, fairly tingling with the life and strength of perfect womanhood; and it may be said that her face was a face to go with one through the years, and to live still in one's dreams when the sap of life is gone, and, withered and old, one sits shaking before the fire; a generous, loving mouth, red lipped, full arched, with the corners tucked in and perfect teeth between; a womanly chin and nose, with character enough to save them from being pretty; hair dark, showing a touch of gold with umber in the shadows; a brow, full broad, set over brown eyes that had never been taught to hide behind their fringed veils, but looked always square out at you with a healthy look of good comradeship, a gleam of mirth, or a sudden, wide, questioning gaze that revealed depth of soul within."

Wright certainly laid it on thick. Romanticized characterizations like that of Sammy Lane were not uncommon in the literature of the day. Clearly Wright had a fascination and considerable admiration for his *Shepherd* characters. All his portrayals were outsized; his heroes were built of positive physical and personal traits; his villains looked and acted wickedly.

Harold Bell Wright was also in love with the environment of the White River Hills. He described in glowing terms the lay of the land and the wonders of the pastoral setting for *The Shepherd of the Hills*. There is no doubt that Wright was sincere in his admiration for the mountainous region and its inhabitants. He would not have called them hillbillies, certainly never in a disparaging way.

Wright's novel and its depictions expressed his own viewpoints. He came from a somewhat difficult, modest background. He respected the exigencies of rural living and appreciated the attributes of the common man. As a minister, he applied moralistic themes to his writing. He attached these themes of good versus evil to the characters and the events that transpire in *The Shepherd* story.

*The Shepherd of the Hills* was wildly popular, becoming one of the most read novels in American literature. It did not matter that Wright was criticized by elite critics. People loved his story. They loved it so much, they wanted to see the hills where it took place and meet the characters he depicted.

With train travel extended through Branson, Missouri by 1906, people came from all over to see and experience the country and the people portrayed in *The Shepherd*. Wright's romanticized novel has attracted millions of visitors to the Branson area for well over one hundred years. His work inspired several movies and an outdoor play that has been performed in Branson since 1960.

Wright's *The Shepherd of the Hills* presented a positive image of the hill people to a large audience. Portrayed as physically strong and morally upright, these fictitious characters, who would be branded by some as hillbillies, were seen in an affirmative manner. Readers of the novel now had a characterization that was admirable and attractive.

*The Shepherd* also established a moralistic or Christian view of the White River Hills inhabitants. This association between the Ozarks hillfolk and Christianity would continue to be applied to some of the presentations of mountain folk by outlanders as well as by locals.

*Cover of Wright's famous book*

There were other forces that would draw Americans to the Ozarks in the early twentieth century. In 1912, Powersite Dam was completed by the Ozark Power and Water Company, damming the White River just upstream from Forsyth. The small lake (twenty- two miles long) transformed the village of Branson into a tourism mecca. People flocked to the resorts and campgrounds on the pretty little lake nestled in the Ozark Mountains.

The tourism industry would continue unabated in the region, supported by float fishing, hunting clubs, sentimentalized promotions by the railroads and land speculators, and glowing romantic novels about the region. The hillbillies of the Ozarks, at least those near tourist destinations, were beginning to learn that their image had commercial appeal. The promotion of mountain crafts, mountain skills, mountain music, and even the comic hillbilly caricature had commercial value. Some of the hillfolk became cooperators in advancing their perceived lifestyle and likeness.

The Country Life Movement arose out of concern for the negative impacts of industrialization and urbanization that was taking place in the United States around the turn of the century. Squalid living conditions, oppressive and dangerous working conditions and jarring poverty were nothing new to man's existence. However, social, religious and moral attitudes were strengthening in response to these perceived evils of the modern world. Academics, politicians and sociologists began to bemoan the negative influences of the cities and extoll the benefits of rural life.

The intention of the Country Life Movement was multi-faceted. America was still a majority agrarian society, but there were disturbing trends. People were moving away from their farms and relocating to the cities. At the same time, large numbers of immigrants were entering the country. Rural America was seen, rightly so, as the producer of food for the growing country. But there were also concerns about the perceived dearth of educational, religious, and social opportunities in the agrarian areas.

Outmigration from agricultural regions could jeopardize food production. There were also racial overtones to these beliefs. To some, the rural population represented a "pure" Anglo-Saxon, white, Protestant stock. "Saving" these "good" people was important to the country's wellbeing and future according to some of the skewed social theories of the time.

So, the Country Life Movement took on two main goals: to improve the lives of rural, farming Americans and encourage the benefits of living on the land and traditional agrarian lifestyles

One of the chief proponents of the movement was Liberty Hyde Bailey. A renowned horticulturist, Bailey was involved in many efforts to promote and improve rural living, including agricultural extension services, 4-H, rural electrification and rural postal delivery. In 1908, President Theodore Roosevelt appointed Bailey to head a Commission on Country Life.

The Movement was plagued by the disparate intentions and ideologies of its various proponents. Involvement of rural people ran the gamut from welcoming acceptance to outright opposition. Some wary rurals viewed the crusade as condescending interference from outside do-gooders.

Ultimately, the Country Life Movement did achieve some success with the establishment of agricultural extension services, improved roads and bridges, and rural health and educational programs.

In the early 1900s, the Country Life Movement continued the conflicted perception of country folk, seen on one hand as valiant and praiseworthy and on the other as backward and needy. Just who were these hillbillies and what were they really like?

The Allen family established a long heritage of rural country living on the Kings River in southern Barry County, Missouri from the late 1800s up to the present.

Blake Allen was the youngest child of Hezekiah (Babe) and Celia (Gibbs) Allen. Blake was born in 1855 in Tennessee and came to Carroll County, Arkansas with his parents as a child. Blake married Sarah Wooley in 1875. By 1880, the Allens were in Barry County, Missouri and by 1884, Blake owned property on the point of land that would eventually bear his name along Kings River.

Blake Allen was an impressive and influential man on the Kings River. He built a two-story log home on his land and over time, increased his property holdings. Blake Allen raised crops and livestock. He ran 300 to 400 hogs that wore his special earmark on the open range. Through hard work, he supported his extended family and aided many neighbors.

To increase the bottomland available for growing crops, Blake Allen built a weir dam out of stone and diverted the Kings toward Jakie Hollow. His efforts opened up another twenty acres of tillable soil on the "bottom slough".

Emmett Allen, Blake's grandson, relates several stories his grandfather told him, sitting out on the porch of their log home on Blake Allen Bluff.

"He said one time over there by Golden, he belonged to what they called the Horse Thieve Antis.[80] They laid over there in the brush one night 'til almost daylight the next morning, waiting for an old boy to come through there. Him and his boys had been out stealin' horses. Just before the break of day, they came across the field there. The field had been cut off and there was just scrub stuff about shoulder high. They stopped 'em. They was just gonna execute 'em on the spot. Everybody kind of felt bad about it. They didn't think the boys would have been doin' it, hadn't been for the old man. So they decided to give 'em a break. They told 'em, "Tell ya what we're gonna do. We're gonna let ya take off runnin'. If ya make it, okay. If ya don't, you've had it." Bless God, you know, both those boys made it. But it looked like everybody in the bunch shot at that old man. They just cut the brush off. You could just see where the shells went toward him instead of toward the boys. Killed the old man. The boys got away."

Blake Allen was known for walking all over the countryside. His back had been injured in a tree-felling accident and he walked with a cane. Nevertheless, Emmett Allen says, as a child, he would have to run to keep up with Blake. Emmett says Blake could get up early, eat breakfast, walk twenty-three miles to Cassville for jury duty, and walk back home in time for supper.

Emmett Allen grew up on the homestead his grandfather Blake Allen established along the Kings River. Emmett was born in the old log cabin in 1929. He describes his early days saying, "We had a window upstairs. Had gunny sacks hangin' over the window. Had a big fireplace across one end of the house. You could fit a four-foot log in that fireplace. We cooked on a wood-stove in a lean-to on the back of the house. We used coal oil lamps. No electricity."

Emmett's parents, Arthur and Annie Allen, had thirteen children, two dying as infants. The large family worked the river bottomlands and ridgeland on the bluff. Emmett says:

"We planted by hand. Plowed by hand with a turnin' plow behind two horses. I walked behind my dad and picked up worms and went fishing for perch. I'd catch a perch and dad would put it on a pole and stick it in the bank. Went down there one morning and I had a catfish bigger than I could carry. I caught a lot of good fish down there. I picked up a lot of arrowheads down there. We planted in April. If it flooded, we replanted. We hoed the Johnson grass out. We planted both directions in a "checked" pattern. It was hard work. We fed the corn to the hogs. It was all free range back then. You marked your livestock with a cut on the ear. Each guy had a brand or special cut mark.

We milked eight or ten old cows. Cut Johnson grass for feed. We cut it by hand, loaded it on a wagon and hauled it up to the barn for feed. We bred work horses. We didn't know what a tractor was. I was seven years old before I saw an automobile. Used to be a grocery store on what is now 39-72. The owner had a 1928 Chevrolet. That was the first one I ever rode in. We had to push him up the hill.

We made our own maple syrup. There was a grove of sugar maples down on the point. In February, we'd drill a hole in the maples with a brace and bit. Tapped the trees and put a bucket on it. After three or four days, we'd bring the buckets up to the house and boil it down to syrup. My Dad was one of the best molasses makers in the country. He planted five or six acres of cane. We stripped the leaves off the cane and cut the tops off. Saved the leaves and tops for livestock feed and seed. We had a horse-operated press mill to get the juice out. Cooked it down to molasses. We sold some and used some.

We had a big vegetable garden. Mom canned and dried foods. We doctored mostly at home. When one of my younger sisters was born, one of my brothers had to go to Grandview to get the doctor. Dad used to fox hunt. He had a hand-made horn he'd blow on the hunts. When Mom went into labor, my brother blew that horn and called Dad in. The doctor showed up the next morning in his buggy. My birth certificate says Golden, but I was born in the log house. People died from typhoid, flu and even malaria back when I was a kid. People used quinine called 'three six chill tonic'. Cost ten or fifteen cents a bottle. You took a spoonful every day to avoid the chills.

I hunted squirrels and rabbits. Used deadfall traps for rabbits. We hunted coons and foxes with dogs. We had mixed-breed hounds — July and Walker. Fox hunting was more of a sport. At night, we'd build a big fire, probably have a little corn whiskey and listen to the dogs run. They could tell by the dogs' calls what they were doing.

When I was a kid, we had a boat made out of a hollow log like a dugout canoe. We nailed some boards in it for seats. We would gig a boatload of fish and eat fish until it was gone. I used to see float trips go by on the river. They'd camp on our bottomland across from Jakie. Mom wouldn't let us go down there because they were drinking and runnin' around naked.

My Dad had a still at Flat Rock Hollow. They kept it a secret. They'd make up a batch of six or eight jugs sometimes. There was a spring in there for their water. Most folks had a still somewhere."

Emmett Allen served in World War II and Korea and was an accomplished boxer as a young man. He recently lived in Cassville with his wife Kathleen where he enjoyed fishing, preserving and cooking food, making wine, and telling stories about life on the Kings River. [81]

The Allen family exhibit many of the positive traits associated with rural living. They made the most of what they had and improved their condition through acquiring and employing sound rugged skills. Their lives may not have been as sentimental as portrayed by Wright and other romanticists, but they certainly were not the crude and comic people lampooned by the Southwestern humorists and the early chroniclers.

The romantics and the rural Arcadians may have softened the image of the hillbilly and garnered attention for the very real problems of rural America, but the mountain people were still often misunderstood or ignored.

Otto Ernest Rayburn has been called a romantic, an Arcadian, a realist and a booster for his many years of writing about the Ozarks. He was all of these and one might include the title regional historian as Rayburn documented considerable folklore and lifeways of the region.

Rayburn, a flatlander from Iowa and Kansas, spent the bulk of his life living, working and studying in the Ozarks. As he traveled around the hills, he set up residences in numerous locations including Reeds Spring, Radical, Kingston, Lonsdale, Galena,

Caddo Gap, Eminence and Eureka Springs. Otto Rayburn admits he was first attracted to the Ozarks region after reading Wright's *The Shepherd of the Hills*. He arrived in 1917 and spent much of the next forty years teaching and writing in his adopted homeland.

Throughout his career, Rayburn kept a positive attitude toward the hillfolk. He lived with them, did business with them and partied with them. He says in his concise autobiography *Forty Years in the Ozarks*: [82]

"I admire the young men of the hills who learn to take care of themselves and do things expertly. In the community where I first pitched my tent, the average young man could plan and construct a log cabin without employing a carpenter. He always shod his own horse, and if he needed a boat, he built it. He could repair a gun, or a pair of shoes, and his barlow knife was always sharp as a razor."

But Rayburn acknowledges some ambiguity in his views when he writes:

"When I wrote the book, *Ozark Country*, for the American Folkways Series in 1940, I was imbued with the spirit of romanticism….I thought this the ideal place to loiter and recuperate, to harness life's forces against civilization's excesses. Nothing is said about the unsanitary conditions of the homesteads that had no back-houses, of the scourge of pellagra due to insufficient or unbalanced diet, or of the ignorance that was rampant because of poor schools and lack of educational facilities. I was looking at the Ozarks through rose colored glasses." [83]

In his later writing, perhaps Rayburn had become more of a realist. However, he was always a booster of the Ozarks. He sincerely loved the environment, the people and the allure of the land he liked to call "Arcadia". His regular newspaper columns "Ozark Folkways" in the *Arkansas Gazette* and "Ozark News Nuggets" for the *Tulsa Tribune*, his magazines *Ozark Life*, *The Arcadian*, *Arcadian Life*, and *Ozark Guide* and his books *Ozark Country* and *Forty Years in the Ozarks* promoted a positive image of the rural Ozarks from the 1920s through the 1950s.

Rayburn was also, perhaps unintentionally, part of the Country Life Movement. He spent six years as School Superintendent at

Kingston, Arkansas. With support from the Presbyterian Board of Missions, Kingston developed a strong community-centered project which included the construction and operation of an educational building, a church and a health center. Despite its isolated locale in the Boston Mountains along the upper reaches of Kings River, the Kingston Community Project successfully combined the resources of the Church, the State of Arkansas and the local citizenry to develop a first-rate school system and community outreach program.

While at Kingston in 1927, Rayburn launched his intent to study, gather and promote Ozarks folklore. He formed the Ozarkians as a literary society and attracted several renowned regional writers and folklorists. This group later combined with the Hillcrofters in 1932. The Ozarkian Hillcrofters borrowed their name from the early Scottish crofts. Their membership included many of the period's Ozarks notables including May Kennedy McCord, Vance Randolph, Dewey Short, Mary Elizabeth Mahnkey, and Rose O'Neill.

The Hillcrofters may not have accomplished much in the way of specific projects, but its membership certainly helped promote a positive image of the Ozarks and generated considerable interest in the region's folkways at a time when these traditions were fading rapidly. (In 2018, the Ozarkian Hillcrofters were re-founded and embarked on several projects to promote and sustain the folkways, history and environment of the Ozarks.)

Rayburn would go on to work as the Arkansas State Historian for the American Legion, President of the Arkansas Folklore Society, and Director of the Ozark Folk Festival in Eureka Springs for five years. Throughout his long career, Otto Rayburn amassed an amazing amount of material on the Ozarks, its unique history, lore and people. In 1955, he began compiling his *Ozark Folk Encyclopedia* to retain the writings, information and stories he had collected over his years in the Ozarks. The compilation (said by Rayburn to contain an estimated 20,000,000 words) is now housed at the Special Collections Library at the University of Arkansas in Fayetteville.

Otto Rayburn's contribution to the understanding and image of the Ozarks should not be underestimated. Through his positive, self-deprecating style and long-time association with the region and its hillfolk, he provided an attractive and generally realistic view of what the Ozarks is all about. Perhaps Rayburn's attitude about his adopted homeland can be surmised from this excerpt from *Forty Years in the Ozarks*: [84]

"Folks who read books and work with machines think of the Hillman as backward, but that is a mistake. When I came to the Ozarks my ability to quote Shakespeare, conjugate verbs and work cube roots, did not help me one bit in locating a bee tree or in taking a boat over Wildcat Shoals. My book knowledge wasn't worth a tinker's dam for practical purposes. I was the backward one, not my neighbors. I would gladly have traded some of Plato's philosophy or Tennyson's poetry for the art of gigging fish in swift water, but no deal. The Hillman matched his environment. I was a misfit. But through perseverance I have learned some of the arts and skills of hill life that have added to my enjoyment. If I ever enter the state of reincarnation, I ask the fates-that-be to favor this one request: 'Make me a hillbilly!'"

You cannot consider yourself a serious student of the Ozarks unless you have read Vance Randolph. Otto Rayburn considered his friend Randolph the "leading Ozark folklorist".[85] Randolph never pulled his punches. He told Ozark stories with humor, first-hand experience, and a blunt reality. He knew his subject and although sometimes accused of embellishment, Randolph did not hesitate to reveal his opinion, be it positive, negative or indifferent.

In his first major work on the subject, *The Ozarks: An American Survival of Primitive Society* (originally published in 1931), Randolph expresses his views on his adopted neighbors, the Ozarks hillbillies, with a mixed assortment of admiration, disgust and fascination. Randolph's interest in the people he referred to as "genuine American" is obvious when he writes: [86]

"There are men in the Ozarks today who sleep in cord beds and hunt with muzzle-loading rifles; there are women who still use spinning-wheels and weave cloth on home-made looms; there are minstrels who sing old English ballads brought over by the seventeenth-century colonists; there are old settlers who believe firmly in witchcraft and all sorts of medieval supersti-

tions; there are people who speak an Elizabethan dialect so outlandish that it is well-nigh unintelligible to the ordinary tourist
from Chicago and points east. The typical Ozark native differs
so widely from the average urban American that when the latter
visits the hill country he feels himself among an alien people.
The Hillman recognizes the difference, too, and refers to all outsiders as 'furriners', whether they come from North Dakota or
South Germany."

In this passage, Vance Randolph mentions several topics
that he would research and record in detail. His collection of
traditional Ozarks music, accumulated and recorded over several years, would result in his *Ozark Folk Songs* (published
1946-1950), a monumental four volume assemblage of over 900
ballads and songs. His study of the Ozarkian dialect would result in *Down in the Holler*[87] a masterfully researched work of
Ozarks words and phrases that can be traced to Chaucerian and
Shakespearian English.

Randolph loved the stories and tall tales he heard from his
hillbilly friends. Several of his works concentrate on superstition, humorous anecdotes and ribald yarns. Some of his collected tales were so risque, publication was delayed for years.
*Pissing in the Snow*[88] was completed in 1954, but did not find a
publisher until 1976. *Roll Me in Your Arms* and *Blow the Candle
Out* were published posthumously in the 1990s.[89]

Randolph's bawdy tales represent only a small portion of his
extensive documentation of Ozarks lore and the Ozarks people.
If anything, they only add to the presentation of a culture and
people that hold a uniqueness and yet share a commonality with
other distinct cultural groups. In the Introduction to *Pissing in
the Snow*, Rayna Green writes, "The printing of bawdy lore sep-
arately from other Ozark traditions should not be viewed as any
indication that the presence of the bawdy is more prominent than
any other lore in Ozark life. Randolph says, in his introduction
to the song manuscripts, 'I do not believe that the bawdy ballads
are more common in the Ozarks than elsewhere, or that the hillfolk as a class are especially fond of them.'" [90]

Vance Randolph sometimes clashed with the Ozarks boosters. He presented a real version of the region, warts and all.

The boosters preferred to promote the area as modern and even idyllic. Randolph's intentions were journalistic or academic; the boosters' were economic or romantic. Vance did not have a problem creating interest in the hill country; he just wanted people to have an honest understanding of the culture and people.

In 1934, several local folk festivals were being organized in cities like Rolla, West Plains and Aurora, following a successful two-day show in Eureka Springs. In April of that year, a large crowd of festival promoters assembled in Springfield in preparation for the All-Ozark Festival.

Several of the event supporters were present including May Kennedy McCord, Sarah Gertrude Knott, Geraldine Parker, Bascom Lunsford, Springfield Mayor Harry Durst, and Mr. and Mrs. Vance Randolph. One of the evening's speakers was John T. Woodruff representing the Springfield Chamber of Commerce.

Woodruff proceeded to lambast those who he saw as presenting the Ozarks in a negative light. He criticized Harold Bell Wright, Thames Williamson, author of *The Woods Colt*, and Vance Randolph calling them "a lot of carpetbaggers who have come in here" and saying they "hardly knew a thing". Woodruff was concerned that the folk festivals would present a negative stereotype of the Ozarks saying, "We are hopeful you won't go to St. Louis and stage any rough stuff."

Randolph was taken aback by the attack, but seemed to take the criticism in stride. Woodruff ended up backing down and the festivals were a success. Woodruff may have wanted to avoid what he perceived as a negative portrayal of the Ozarks, but he missed the mark by badmouthing the very people who wanted to present some of the admirable qualities of the Ozarks and its people. The exhibition of the arts and crafts, the music, and the ingenious pioneering skills of the hill country were definitely worth showing off and the folk festivals continued their popularity until the present day. [91]

Randolph at times also lamented what he saw as the gradual loss of the real hillbilly and his unique lifestyle. In *The Ozarks*, Randolph writes: [92]

"I do not pretend to know what is to become of these people, but I cannot believe that, as a class, they will be able to adapt themselves to the complex requirements of modern civilization, or that they will ever again play any important part in the development of the region in which they live. It may be that the native Ozarkers will soon give place to 'furriners', and vanish like the Indians and the Bluff Dwellers who kept these wilds in other years. If the Ozark hill-billy has done his work and outlived his usefulness, he must inevitably go the way of all primitive people who stand in the way of economic progress. To those of us who know the old-timers, however, the transition is not without a touch of melancholy and regret. The valleys raise corn, perhaps, but the Ozark hills produced extraordinary men and women. Their passing definitely closes one of the most romantic and colorful chapters in the history of our country."

Randolph was correct. The impact of modernization, progress, tourism and commercialization would slowly erode the mountain folks' isolated lifestyle. A "primitive" people untouched by the modern world was a fading image even when he wrote these words in 1931. Randolph would do his part to at least document the Ozarks folkways. He supported preservation of the mountain lore and skills that he admired not only through his considerable body of written and recorded work, but also through his efforts with the Ozarkian Hillcrofters and the Ozark Folk Festivals. Randolph told Clay Anderson in 1979, "Everything that I wrote about the Ozarks, I took seriously." [93]

*Vance Randolph at his Pineville Cabin 1927*

The work of writers like Wright, Rayburn and Randolph was notable in its preservation of Ozarks traditions and lore. They impacted the image of the hillbilly through their personal associations with mountain folk and documentation of their interactions. But whether the romantic image portrayed by Wright, the benevolent view expressed by Rayburn, or the realistic accounts of Randolph, their descriptions were up against a new wave of hillbilly personae developing in popular culture. Music and movies could reach a massive audience and the mountain man and mountain maid would be common subjects in these art forms.

# Chapter 4

## Country Folk and Hillbillies

*Vineta Jane (Terherst) Wingate* grew up in the Denver and Enon area. She was born near Denver, Arkansas in 1949. Her parents Glenford Terherst and Nellie (Peden) Terherst sharecropped a farm on Long Creek growing corn and watermelons and raising cattle. The Terhersts had horses, pigs and chickens and a huge vegetable garden. Vineta had seven siblings. She went to elementary school at Farewell.

Vineta did housework, tended her younger sisters and helped with farm chores. There was no electricity at her family's place until 1962. The Terhersts had kerosene lanterns for lights and heated with wood. Milk was kept cool by placing it in a cistern. Later, they had a cookstove and refrigerator fueled by butane. Water was drawn by hand from a drilled well. There was no indoor plumbing. "I never had indoor plumbing until I left home," Vineta relates. "I got married in 1968. My parents still did not have indoor plumbing. When we bought grandpa's farm in 1963, there was a drilled well there with an electric pump. We had power through REA. You had to take your bucket and go out to the little wellhouse, flip the electric switch and hold your bucket there and then carry your bucket into the house." Vineta says they ran water to the kitchen in 1964. Her parents put in a bathroom in 1968. The Terhersts got their first telephone in 1966.

Vineta's family purchased her grandfather Will Terherst's farm near Enon in 1963. They established a substantial dairy cow operation on the mostly cleared rolling hills above Long

Creek. Initially, they milked by hand, but purchased electric milking machines by 1964. Milk was stored in a concrete tank and sold to regional wholesalers.

They often used a team of horses and a wagon on the farm. "I can remember going to the cane field and loading a shock of cane into the wagon with the team of horses and feeding it to the cows. My dad always liked to plow the garden behind a team. We got a tractor when we lived at Denver."

Vineta says, "We were too busy tryin' to make a livin' to have fun. We went to church and worked and went to school. We went to church about seven days a week. We went to a Pentecostal Church. Sometimes mom would load us kids up in the trailer and drive the tractor to church. There was a piano at church. Somebody would have an accordion and a guitar." Vineta says for fun she and her brothers and sisters would scrape "roads" in the barnlot and run up and down the "roads" like they were "cars".

"I lived in the creek. During the summer, we went to Long Creek a lot. Close to our house was a shoal. During the summer, we bathed in the creek. There was a swimming hole. If mom would let us, we'd go to Denver and go to Blue Hole. That was 'the place to go'. It has always been special. Still is today. It was a deep hole about 20 feet deep with a rock wall on one side. Everybody went. It's still a popular place today."

Vineta recalls fishing for perch in the creek. Her dad fished some; he was usually too busy trying to make a living. Glenford fished for catfish and suckers. He liked to snag suckers in the spring. The suckers were gutted, scaled, sliced and fried. If Glenford brought in a good catch in a 'tow' sack, Nelly would prepare and can the fish. In the winter, the preserved suckers made delicious fish patties.

Mrs. Wingate reminisces, "We canned lots of everything. My father was a very good provider for his family. We always had plenty, plenty to eat. My mother was a hard worker and pre-served everything. We ate like kings. I didn't know it at the time, but I look back now and nobody was going hungry. Always meat, vegetables, milk, cream, eggs. Our cellar was full of everything. We bought flour, sugar, salt, baking powder and coffee at the general store."

The Terhersts did their doctoring at home. Vineta remembers never having a doctor come to their house. Nelly used kerosene as a cure-all. When her brother was bitten on the hand by a copperhead, his hand was placed in kerosene. When the milkman showed up at their place, he took Nelly and her son to Denver and then on to Green Forest where they saw a physician.

Childbirth was assisted by a midwife. Maude Avery was the midwife around Denver for many years. Maude helped deliver Vineta in 1949, her sister in 1951 and several others after that. Vineta's grandmother Vineta Hopper Peden was a midwife near Enon for several years. She charged two dollars for a delivery. Midwives were required to fill out a birth certificate for each birth and send it to Little Rock. Vineta says, "They were just ladies that knew what they were doing."

In 1955, Glenford Terherst got a job working on Table Rock Dam. He worked as a concrete finisher's helper. He had to join the union and made $1.25- 1.35 an hour. Vineta remembers, "That was good cash money. My father thought he'd died and gone to heaven." Glenford worked long hours on the dam with only an occasional layoff. When Table Rock was completed, he worked on the Beaver Dam project.

After purchasing Vineta's grandfather's farm on Long Creek in 1963, Nellie Terherst ran the Holstein dairy operation. Glenford worked on the Beaver Dam. When the dam project was finished, he went to work for Tyson at night and worked the farm during the day. Vineta says, "We all worked very hard."

"When I grew up there it was quiet. I have pleasant memories as a child near Denver. There was always coming and going and people. Activities. At Enon, as a teenage girl, I felt I was left out. There wasn't anywhere to go. I felt trapped. I was not allowed to get to the world. It was an ideal place, but a "prison" to a teenager. It was a long ways from nowhere to Enon." [94]

Sanford Garland was born at home in 1931 near Viola, Missouri to Joseph Theodore Garland and Bernice (Willyard) Garland. Sanford's maternal great-grandfather was Lewis Henry Willyard. Lewis homesteaded land along what is now Highway

39 from the present site of Greenshores up to Viola and on both sides of the Kings River in 1891. Sanford's maternal grandmother was Olive McKee. The McKees ran a general store and mill in Viola in the late 1800s and early 1900s. The McKee Mill was a large, steam-powered mill that served the region for many years until it burned down.

McKee's store was situated just west of the Baptist Church. The church was built in 1884 and still stands today. The stone exterior was added later by Joseph Garland. Grant McKee operated the mill which was located just west of the general store. The mill ran on power supplied from a large steam engine. Water for the steam engine came from a spring behind the mill. This spring still feeds three small consecutive ponds.

Sandy Garland grew up around the family home on Couch Bend (now Greenshores Development) about one mile northwest of Viola. The Couch family also owned property in this area. The Garlands ran dairy and Black Angus cattle on their farm. They sold their raw milk to the Pet Milk Company in ten-gallon milk cans, which were picked up daily. If the milk got "blinky" or slightly soured, dairy farmers would sometimes add baking soda to "sweeten" the milk. Sanford's wife Arlene, who grew up in nearby Shell Knob, recalls that the milk company started putting red dye in any slightly soured milk and returned the product to the dairy farmer. Many families would use this dyed milk for personal use. Arlene says, "We grew up thinking cottage cheese was supposed to be pink."

When he was a teenager, Sanford's family moved closer to Viola and he helped at the general store. He roamed the hills and hollers along the Kings River, hunting squirrels and exploring the old bluff shelters along the river. Sanford says, "You could walk across the Kings at the shoals. The water was very clear. We'd ford the river out at the end of the point and climb up to Couch Spring on Stillhouse Bluff. Sometimes we'd put melons in the spring to keep them cold."

Sandy Garland liked to fish the river. He had a johnboat made of pine about twenty feet long and three feet wide in the center, with a squared off bow and stern. The ends of the float boat were tapered in and raked upward. The boat was painted and tarred on the bottom. This type of craft was very stable and worked well for gigging. Sandy gigged suckers, catfish and bass from his boat using a long-handled gig.

Sanford's father was the mail carrier out of Viola from 1945 to 1967. Sandy tells of how he had to fill in for his father on one occasion:

"Now when I was sixteen years old, I got my driver's license. My mother was seriously ill and was in the hospital in Springfield. My dad stayed up there. You had to be at least eighteen to be a substitute mail carrier. So I couldn't carry the mail. I had a sister who was older than me and she could carry the mail. But she didn't drive. So I drove and she carried the mail. We did that during one of the worst ice storms we've ever had in this part of the country."

During Sanford's youth, Viola was a thriving little town with two general stores and three churches (including the Baptist and Church of Christ). Like many small towns of the era, Viola had a baseball team. Managed by Doc Kelley, they played teams from other small towns, but never on Sundays. Sandy recalls, "On Sunday, everybody went to church."

Before World War II, Viola had telephone service, but no electricity. The Garlands heated with wood and used kerosene or gasoline lamps for lighting. Water was drawn from a well by hand. Dairy farmers like the Garlands milked by hand until the coming of REA (Rural Electrification Administration) allowed the installation of milking machines.

Arlene (Cooper) Garland recalls the nature of healthcare when she was growing up. "I can remember mother when I got the croup. She'd take a spoonful of sugar and take the wick out of the kerosene lamp and drip some kerosene into that spoon. And I had to swallow that medicine."

Sanford and Arlene Garland were married in 1950. They relocated to Kansas City, but returned to their Ozarks roots and now reside in the spacious home they built on property west of Shell Knob, once owned by "Wild Bill" Hickok and later by Arlene's family, the Whismans. [95]

Today, there is little evidence of the town of Viola. The Viola Baptist Church is the most visible reminder of the community that once thrived here. But you can imagine where the big mill sat. Perhaps you can visualize the assorted merchandise stacked around the pot-bellied stove at the general store or imagine the crack of a bat as Alan Hale of the Viola baseball team hit a homerun.

*McKee Store at Viola*

In his comprehensive book, *Hillbilly A Cultural History of an American Icon*, Anthony Harkins clearly states how the hillbilly's dual image prevailed throughout the entire twentieth century: [96]

"Although the hillbilly image has remained relatively unchanged, the meaning of these representations and the word itself have continuously evolved over the past century in response to broader social, economic, and cultural transformations in American society. The key to the 'hillbilly's' surprising ubiquity and endurance from 1900 to the dawn of the third millennium has been the fundamental ambiguity of the meaning of this term and image."

Beginning with the romantic portrayals of Ozarks mountain people and the Country Life Movement, the 20th century would bring an abundance of crusades to improve the lives and economic condition of the country folk of the Ozarks region. The Great Depression certainly brought attention to the poverty and lack of modern resources available for these folk. The forests and waterways of the Ozarks would also attract considerable interest. Much of this attention came from the State and Federal governments. Church groups and the town elites of Ozarks cities wanted to help, too. The mountain people viewed these benevolent ventures with a mixture of gratitude, ambiguity and outright disdain.

Dewey Jackson Short hailed from Galena, the small James River town and county seat of Stone County, Missouri, once touted as "the float fishing capital of the world". The Short family were respected citizens and could probably be considered town elites. May Kennedy McCord described Dewey at an early age:

"Just an unsophisticated Hillbilly with no reserved seat in the King's Court, yet the boy seemed destined from the start to have a luminous place somewhere in the mosaic of life." [97]

Dewey followed the tenets held dear by many Ozarkers, receiving a stellar education, studying and practicing in the ministry, staying close to his roots, and clinging to an independent streak. His greatest skill was speaking, earning him the moniker, "orator of the Ozarks". Dewey employed his gift of discourse well, translating it into a long career in politics. He served twelve terms in the U.S. House of Representatives between 1929 and 1957.

But Dewey Short also exhibited what may appear to be some contradictions. Although committed to the welfare of his constituents, he fought bitterly against the Federal programs of the New Deal. Despite the popularity and positive impact of programs like the CCC and WPA on the Ozarks region, Short lambasted Roosevelt's work to lift the country out of the Depression as government overreach. He commented in the House of Representatives in 1939 concerning appropriations for the WPA:

"These new dealers are liberal with the other guy's dough, but even an Ozark hillbilly where I reside has enough hard common sense to know that Santa Claus really does not come down the chimney the night before Christmas, that the Easter eggs are not laid by bunny rabbits, that no government can ever give to its people anything it does not take from them, and that eventually they must foot the bill. He who dances must pay the fiddler,,," [98]

Short may have been dubious about big government programs, but he certainly got behind the massive Corps of Engineers projects to tame the White River. He knew these projects would help alleviate regional flooding and provide an economic boon to his district. But he also had to know that many people would lose their bottomland to eminent domain and these folk were not at all happy about that.

Representative Short fought hard to achieve passage of the Flood Control Act of 1941 which resulted in the eventual impoundment of all of the White River in Missouri. The Dewey Short Visitor Center at Table Rock Dam is named in his honor.

Another contradiction associated with Dewey Short revolves around his brother. Leonard Short, often known as "Shock" to those who knew him well, took a much different path than his famous sibling. Well-liked by the people of Stone County, Leonard seemed fun-loving and gregarious, but could not avoid serious trouble. In 1933, Shock was acquitted of complicity in a robbery of the Bank of Galena. The following year he was convicted of a bank robbery in Oklahoma and sentenced to a term in the penitentiary. In December 1935, Leonard escaped from the jail in Muskogee, but died from exposure on the cold Oklahoma plains.

Of course, Dewey cannot be blamed for the behavior of his brother. But the stories of these two men provide an interesting contrast in the image of Ozarks folk. In his eloquent and humorous speaking style, Dewey Short proclaimed his tongue-in-cheek pride in his mountain ancestry: [99]

"Really, I am just a plain, ordinary, country boy, a native hillbilly from the Ozarks in southwest Missouri, where we still cover our houses with bull hides and use their tails for lightning rods."

*Cover of Wiley's book*

While Dewey Short railed against the New Deal, the Ozarks was in trouble. On top of serious drought conditions, years of poor agricultural practices contributed to reduced crop yields. What could be harvested faced plummeting prices. Decades of overharvesting of forests, wildlife and fisheries were detrimental to the entire landscape.

Even the isolated hillfolk, who may not even had known they were poor, faced destitution. Many Ozarkers turned to migrant labor, traveling regionally or as far as the West coast during harvest season to earn cash money working the large farms, orchards and ranches. Like the "Okies" from drought stricken Oklahoma, some country folk gave up their homesteads and moved away forever. This outmigration left the Ozark region even more sparsely populated.

The 1930s did see attempts to alleviate some of these problems. The Rural Electrification Administration began to bring power to the rural Ozarks. The Works Progress Administration provided jobs for many Ozarkers and constructed buildings and infrastructure that still exist today. The Civilian Conservation Corps put thousands of young men to work building roads, fighting fires, planting trees and creating parks.

The Missouri Department of Conservation was established in 1937 and began its mission of protecting and improving the State's natural resources. The Ozarks National Forest was established in Arkansas in 1908. The Mark Twain and Clark National Forests in Missouri were founded in 1939. These massive wooded areas of the Ozarks were protected or at least managed in a way that would ensure their growth and continued existence as forest lands.

The Depression era was tough on everyone. The hillbilly image was cast against the background of widespread poverty and class distinctions. The realist view of the mountain people took on a more pronounced role. One of the fictional works that captured national attention was *The Woods Colt* by Thames Williamson. [100]

*The Woods Colt* is a fast-paced, well written, realistic novel set in the Arkansas Ozarks. Williamson was a prolific, talented writer who published several novels, often with settings in unique sub-cultures. He was not particularly kind to the mountain people he characterized in *The Woods Colt* (woods colt is a rural euphemism for a child born out of wedlock). In fact, all of the novel's characters are portrayed primarily with negative traits. The novel is exciting and even surprisingly erotic. The woodcut illustrations by Raymond Bishop are excellent depictions of the book's scenes.

Harold Bell Wright's romanticized depiction of Sammy Lane in the *The Shepherd of the Hills* is in sharp contrast to how Williamson realistically describes Clint Morgan's (the woods colt) mother: [101]

"The cords stand out on her hands, big wide hands, brown an' hard. Black hair like Clint's, only stiffer and wilder. And eyes that you better not git in the way of, or they'll burn a hole in ye, same as a coal o' fire. Come right down to it, you'd never believe she ever turned any feller's head at a brush-arbor meetin', moon or no moon. Maw shore done it, though. That's how she come by her woods colt. She was young, and the preacher was shoutin' about salvation not more'n a gunshot away, so Uncle Darby says. Clint looks at her. Well, she's chawin' terbaccer, an' somethin' else besides, by the way her jaws grind together. Long green ain't so tough as all that."

The Woods Colt is written almost entirely in dialect. Perhaps there is too much vernacular, but the book does flow smoothly and one cannot doubt Williamson's commitment to authenticity as he claims Vance Randolph reviewed his manuscript twice for language accuracy. The story uses almost every negative stereotype associated with the hill people: violent men, bawdy women, corncob pipe-smoking grannies, moonshiners, long-barrel rifles, hound dogs, feuds, superstitions, corn pone and run-down log cabins.

There are few references to more positive cultural traits, with the exception of maybe the characters' hunting and tracking skills. Williamson uses the term "hillbilly" a handful of times (and "brush apes" once). The context is generally between the hillfolk themselves, but carries a derogatory meaning. Williamson is kinder to the Ozarks landscape. His depictions of the hills, hollows and streams seem authentic and complimentary.

His realistic story does seem to be fairly well-informed. The descriptions of home life, noodling a catfish, sucker grabbing and using horns for communication are faithful and veritable. It is unclear how Williamson obtained his research for *The Woods Colt*. He does not appear to have spent any great length of time in the Ozarks. However, he was certainly acquainted with Randolph and says in the book's dedication that "we traveled them thar hills together". Williamson was a top notch researcher and writer who could put together a good story and keep it believable. Like all novelists, Thames Williamson was writing for an audience. His intent must have been to entertain and not necessarily to inform.

Nevertheless, *The Woods Colt* does feed the perception that the Ozarkers were a singular society of brutish outliers. *The Woods Colt* was another publication by an outlander that presented a realistic, but mostly negative view of the Ozarks folk. Maybe Williamson's accomplished novel (it was suggested for a Pulitzer Prize by a *Time* magazine writer) gives a view of the mountain people that although based in reality is limited. Perhaps it presents an impression that is somewhat like a scene in the story. Clint, the woods colt, hears his girlfriend Tillie talking to someone in her cabin. He digs some of the chinking out between the cabin's logs and peers inside. He partially sees Tillie completely nude and assumes she is cheatin' on him. He rushes inside to find that she is alone and was talking to herself while trying on a new dress.

Clint made an assessment based on a limited view and incomplete information. *The Woods Colt* is a wonderful tale and well-told, but it only provides a peek at the mountain culture and it mostly ignores the region's more admirable qualities.

If anyone knew and portrayed the hillbilly of the Ozarks in a realistic style, it was Vance Randolph. His work was so well researched and presented with such honesty that it is hard to disagree with his judgements. If one chose to quibble, perhaps one could argue that Randolph was an outsider, even though he spent the bulk of his life living in the Ozark Mountains. He also wrote to entertain and has been accused of the occasional embellishment. But in the final analysis, Vance Randolph was so immersed in Ozarks culture that his writings and recordings have to be considered a permanent, accurate compilation of all things hillbilly.

Randolph accumulated a treasure trove of Ozarks music. Many of the songs he heard and recorded were the traditional mountain folksongs which had their source in Anglo-Saxon and Celtic music. These ancient melodies crossed the Atlantic Ocean, entered the Piedmont and Appalachia regions, traveled westward into Kentucky and Tennessee and finally made their way into the Ozarks.

Are these songs the basis for what some would refer to as hillbilly music? Or did the hillbilly sound develop as a separate genre, created out of a commercial interest in several styles of rural music? The traditional melodies were the ballads and airs that the mountain people had learned from their ancestors and held in their hearts. The hillfolk were passionate about retaining the tunes and lyrics in the exact way they had been learned. Each person held that their songs were true to the original version. It was old music that despite the singers' and musicians' efforts had been slowly changed over the centuries.

Vance Randolph says in *Ozark Mountain Folks*: [102]

"I have never known a genuine backwoods ballad-singer who did not insist upon this meticulous accuracy; they all sing their songs exactly as they learned them, and bitterly resent any tinkering or 'improvement' of either text or melody."

*Vance Randolph recording Ozarks music*

But there were many versions, some slightly modified, others considerably altered. Through time and travel, individuals made up their own words or added a minor musical flourish. The hillfolks' music was meant to be faithful to its origins, but like all art forms, it couldn't resist influences, even in the isolated mountain regions. Vance Randolph documents fifteen variations on *Barbara Allen* alone in his massive collection of Ozarks folk songs.[103] Other folklorists have collected and recorded dozens more versions of the seventeenth century British ballad.

Innovation and modification crept in from many sources: the songs of the French voyageurs, the South's slaves, the non-English speaking immigrants, the Protestant hymns, the Native Americans, the minstrels, and the traveling troubadours were heard. Subtle influences slipped in.

The musical instruments of the mountain people also influenced and changed the traditional art form. Frequently, these songs were sung unaccompanied. But very often, they were aided by the fiddle, the banjo, or the guitar. These stringed instruments could also be handmade and many were. They were the most common instruments, although by no means the only ones. Musical instruments were a luxury item for many, so some were less common in the hills. The mandolin, autoharp, dulcimer, piano and organ were all present and had their impact on this folk music.

The fiddle may be the most ubiquitous instrument in hillbilly music. With ancient origins, the violin passed through centuries of use in all types of music. Light and relatively small, the fiddle found extensive use in the mountain enclaves. A good fiddler could provide lively jig tunes, spirited dance music or somber ballads. Some of those with a religious bent eschewed the fiddle as "an instrument of the devil," but most of the mountain folk appreciated its importance to their culture.

***Dancing at an Ozark Picnic***

"The Mountain Whippoorwill" (subtitled "Or, How Hill-Billy Jim Won the Great Fiddler's Prize"), a poem by acclaimed writer Stephen Vincent Benet, is a wonderful story carrying the mystique and importance of the fiddle in mountain culture. Written in 1925, "The Mountain Whippoorwill" tells the tale of a young mountain lad entering and winning a fiddle contest. With appropriate use of vernacular and graceful phrasing, Benet's poem captures the joy, thrill and sadness that the mountain fiddle could impart.

Perhaps the instrument that has had the most unique influence on hillbilly music is the banjo. The banjo is a distinctly American instrument in its present form. It was originally developed by African slaves recreating the gourd "banja" of West Africa. The instrument was co-opted by minstrel shows in the early 1800s and became intertwined with rural mountain music.

Variations of the banjo's unique sound and playing styles impacted the performance of the traditional Ozarks mountain music. Finger picking, strumming or clawhammer styles lent a new and different sound to the old ballads.

Hillbilly music developed in the mountains and retained some elements of Scots-Irish tradition. But it could not avoid outside influences. Even by the 1930s when John and Alan Lomax and Vance Randolph began recording traditional mountain music, the effects of phonographs, radio and movies had begun to seep into the hill country. Intercultural crossover would only accelerate the evolution of hillbilly music. Brooks Blevins says in *Hill Folks A History of Arkansas Ozarkers & Their Image*: [104]

"Ballad collectors [of the 1930s] found in the region a wealth of folk songs, but they also discovered what [Thomas Hart] Benton discovered: that the region was in a state of flux and that even traditional music was beginning to be eschewed by a younger generation to whom radios and phonographs had delivered the commercial sounds of Nashville, Chicago, or New Orleans."

The music of the hillfolk began to receive national attention during the 1920s. Phonograph record producers and radio show developers found a lively market for "old time" music. Unsure what to call these country musicians, music producers sought out performers with repertoires of traditional and folk tunes. Archie Green says in "Hillbilly Music: Source and Symbol", "It is my thesis that the term *hillbilly music* was born out of the marriage of a commercial industry — phonograph records and some units of show business — with traditional Appalachian folksong." [105]

Okeh Records had success with so-called "race" recordings starting in 1921. Okeh executive Ralph Peer travelled to Atlanta in 1923 to seek out new talent and ended up recording Fiddlin' John Carson. Carson was from the Blue Ridge Mountains of Georgia. He had learned to fiddle at an early age on his grandfather's violin — a Stradivarius copy dated 1714, reputedly brought to the north Georgia hills from Ireland in 1780. [106]

Fiddlin' John worked at a variety of manual jobs and played his fiddle at every opportunity he could find. In 1923, Okeh recorded Carson playing "The Little Old Log Cabin in the Lane", "The Old Hen Cackled", and "The Rooster's Going to Crow". These recordings sold well and Peer realized the potential of music that came from and was appreciated by a rural market. Fiddlin' John Carson's success opened up a profusion of interest in old time and folk music. [107]

In July, 1924, record company Vocalian recorded talented musician "Uncle" Dave Macon singing "Hill Billie Blues", probably a reconstruction of "Hesitation Blues". It is considered the first record label to use the term "hill billie". [108]

Recording studios and record companies were unsure what to call this mountain music, but they realized its commercial potential. At a session in 1925 at Okeh Records in New York, a four-man string band from Virginia was asked by recording executive Ralph Peer what their band's name was. One of the members, Al Hopkins replied, "Call us anything you want. We're nothing but a bunch of hillbillies from North Carolina and Virginia anyway!" Peer instructed the New York Okeh studios secretary to write Hill Billies in the ledger. [109]

In his comprehensive analysis of the origins of the "hillbilly" music genre, Archie Green wrote in the *Journal of American Folklore*, "So long as we both exploit and revive hillbilly music, so long as we feel tension between rural and urban society, we are likely to continue to need Ralph Peer's and Al Hopkins' jest." [110]

Dr. Henry Harlin Smith held a fiddling contest in Calico Rock, Arkansas in 1926 to promote the positive aspects of the region. The five winners of the contest were formed into a string band named the Hoss-Hair Pullers. Smith combined the Hoss-Hair Pullers with four area vocalists, the Hill-Billy Quartet. Various combinations of these musicians performed on a series of Hot Springs radio broadcasts and recorded six songs in 1928 on the Victor label.[111]

The six recorded tunes reveal a mixture of musical influences. Fiddles are prominent with the use of banjo and guitar providing rhythm. The hymn "Up in Glory" is accompanied by a lone mandolin. The voices are all two- or three-part male harmonies.

"Going Down the River" is the closest the Hoss Hair Pullers came to a truly traditional piece. "Just Give Me the Leavings", "Save My Mother's Picture from the Sale", and "In the Garden Where the Irish Potatoes Grow" are late 19th or early 20th century commercial tunes. "Ni--er Baby" rose from the exploitive minstrel show genre.

Dr. Smith hoped that the musicians he put together would represent the unique talent of the isolated Ozarks. But the songs they played and recorded clearly show they were already significantly influenced by more mainstream culture. The Hoss Hair Pullers and Hillbilly Quartet did have a sound that would be heard and popularized as "hillbilly", "bluegrass", or "country" music. The sound, style and appearance of these musical groups would play a major role in the image and judgements of the Ozarks and its people.

It is interesting to note that in some of their publicity images, The Hill Billies presented very different impressions. In a pen and ink drawing used in Okeh's 1925 record catalog, the Hill Billies are shown as well-dressed, well-manicured musicians with piano, fiddle, guitar and banjo. In a period photo, the group is seen dressed in overalls, floppy hats and neck scarves. They appear to be singing and present a much more "country" and casual appearance. Perhaps the record executives did not quite know what to do with these fellows. What they did discover was that this type of music was popular and had a lucrative market.

OKeh "OLD TIME" TUNES

THE HILL BILLIES

| 40336<br>10 in. .75 | CRIPPLE CREEK, Orchestra, Vocal Chorus by Al. Hopkins<br>The Hill Billies |
|---|---|
| | SALLY ANN, Orchestra, Vocal Chorus by Al. Hopkins<br>The Hill Billies |

*The Hill Billies*

151

The songs of the mountain folk had been discovered, but it was being sloshed around in a mixture of all types of music. Derogatory perceptions of the hillbilly label and combinations with tunes from a plethora of sources — cowboy songs, spirituals, minstrel ditties, sea shanties, work songs, and folk music — muddied the musical waters. Archie Green writes, "In 1930, Bradley Kincaid, a fine Kentucky folksinger and early record and radio interpreter of traditional material, wrote to his audience: [112]

'There is a practice among recording companies, and those who are inclined to speak slightly of the mountain songs, to call them Hilly Billy songs. When they say Hilly Billy songs they generally mean bum songs and jail songs... [These] are not characteristic of mountain songs, and I hope... you will come to distinguish between these fine old folk songs of the mountains, and the so-called Hilly Billy songs.'"

This "hillbilly" music coming out of the Appalachian and Ozarks regions would achieve extensive national attention through the *Grand Ole Opry*. In the fall of 1925, a small Nashville radio station WSM started broadcasting and soon developed its banner weekly show, *Barn Dance*, which would become the *Grand Ole Opry*.

The first musical guest on the show was old-time music fiddler "Uncle Jimmy" Thompson. He set a tone for the style and presentation of acts on the *Opry*. Thompson was talented and could play scores of tunes he had learned in Tennessee and Texas. His eccentric personality established a trend leading to the skits, comedy routines and musical performances that became so popular to listeners of the show.

George D. Hay, founder and long-time announcer for the Opry radio show said in his *A Story of the Grand Ole Opry*: [113]

"We never use the word [hillbilly] because it was coined in derision. Furthermore, there is no such animal. Country people have a definite dignity of their own and a native shrewdness which enables them to hold their own in any company. Intolerance has no place in our organization and is not allowed."

Meanwhile, in the Ozarks, two women were demonstrating the strength and wisdom of the rural hillfolk. Mary Elizabeth

Mahnkey wrote beautiful, inspiring stories of her life in and around Taney County, Missouri and May Kennedy McCord applied her musical and writing talents to promote the Ozarks and its people.

May Kennedy was born in Carthage, Missouri and spent her formative years in Galena. She married into the prominent Stone County McCord family and eventually moved to Springfield where she would live out her long, influential life.

May Kennedy McCord became known as the "Queen of the Hillbillies" and she wore her title as a badge of honor. She said, "I'm of his tribe and his clan and I love every bone in his body. And if I or any contributor of mine ever mis-represent the Hillbilly may the blackness of the desert hide us, the sand fleas devour us and our bones bleach till the judgment day." [114]

May wrote her weekly "Hillbilly Heartbeats" article for the Springfield News and Leader starting in 1932. From 1938 to 1942, her commentary was published three times a week in the Springfield Daily News. Her writing was inspirational, humorous and entertaining. She wrote of the daily joys and sorrows of the mountain people. McCord solicited stories and comments from her readers and often included these personal anecdotes in her column. In the 1940's, May recorded her "Hillbilly Heartbeats" show on KWK radio in St. Louis. In her pleasant, lilting voice, May spoke of the rustic man, the country boy, the mountain lass, and especially of the proud woman of the hills.

May McCord often wrote and lectured about the cultural changes impacting the rural Ozarks. She admired the skills and hard work it took to maintain a good life in the hills and hollows. Sometimes she bemoaned the slow passing of the "old ways" and the loss of the homespun crafts, the appreciation of simple pleasures, and the "primitive" skills it took to survive in the Ozarks country.

The "troubadour of the Ozarks" was instrumental in establishing regional folk festivals that demonstrated and helped preserve the mountain ways. She was particularly interested in traditional music, recruiting local musical talent for regional festivals and recording many old tunes herself, several of which are retained in the Library of Congress.

Vocalizing in her hauntingly clear voice and accompanying herself on the piano or more often her "old black guitar", May loved to sing the folk songs, the old Scottish/English ballads like *Barbry Allen* or *The Wife of Usher's Well*. She enjoyed the play party tunes like *Rolly Trudum* that she learned as a young lass in Galena and the more recent folk songs like *Jesse James*. Although its actual provenance is unknown, May is sometimes credited for the origin of *The Palace Grand*, a song she performed in the style of the old English ballads. [115]

Along with her friends Vance Randolph, Otto Rayburn, Dewey Short, and Rose O'Neill, May Kennedy McCord was one of the founding members of the Ozarkian Hillcrofters. The Hillcrofters used their extensive knowledge of everything Ozarks and their national audience to promote a positive image of the hillbilly and their mountain culture.

May Kennedy McCord employed her voice to champion the hillbilly image and present a positive portrait of the people and the rolling hills and shadowed dales of her homeland. For nearly five decades she spoke to her folk and the conscience of America until her last farewell, "God willin' and the creek don't rise". [116]

***May Kennedy McCord 1934***

Flowing out of Arkansas, Long Creek meandered north until it spilled into the White River. Just above this confluence, the village of Cedar Valley nestled along the stream below the rise of Goat Hill. In the early twentieth century, the post office took a new name and the hamlet became known as Oasis.

Oasis was indeed a watery sanctuary in the rugged White River Hills with its grist mill, modest homes and hardworking citizens. The following quote from *A Candle Within Her Soul* by Ellen Gray Massey describes the scene: [117]

"A row of catalpa trees lined the lane from the store to the large red barn. Willows and other trees formed a narrow border on either side of Long Creek as it made a big bend around the valley to the mill where it turned north to disappear into forested bluffs."

In 1922 C.P. and Mary Elizabeth Mahnkey purchased the Oasis mill and store and operated them until 1935. The Mahnkeys worked hard to make a living and raise their family during these "hard" times. The blacksmith shop and sawmill were operated by C.P.'s brother Bill. The Mahnkeys built and rented out three cabins along the creek to early tourists to the area.

Mary Elizabeth Mahnkey was a prolific writer of poems, stories and articles. Her insightful understanding of real people and life in the Ozarks shines through her work. Her writings introduced many Americans to the beauty and mystery of these hills and helped found the Taneyhills Library in Branson.

Mahnkey was a voracious reader and started writing at the early age of fourteen. From 1891 until her death in 1948, Mary wrote nearly 3000 columns that were published in local, regional and national magazines and newspapers. She spent almost her entire life in Taney County, Missouri where she lived a simple, honest life as a mother, wife and business proprietor.

Mahnkey wrote both prose and poetry. KWTO radio of Springfield, Missouri named her "Poet Laureate of the Ozarks" for 1943, a title she clearly deserved for her lifetime commitment to describing the simple and yet profound beauty of her homeland. She spoke of the humble things of life and the world around her — wildflowers, housecleaning, cooking and illness. Her unaffected, direct style is revealed in one of her poems:[118]

"I have found beauty
In commonplace things,
In a blue gingham apron
With crisply tied strings,
In freshly washed windows,
With checked curtains brief,
In the mottled rose gray
Of a frost-bitten leaf,
Ruby red velvet
In a tiny toad stool,
Silky green plush
In a polliwog pool."

In 1935, Mary Elizabeth was honored as the best rural correspondent in the United States and Canada by the Croswell Publishing Company and received a trip to New York City. The national attention brought her descriptions of Ozarks life to a wide audience, an audience that had not heard much from an actual Ozarker, an Ozarker who presented a true, honest, beautiful portrait of mountain people and their respectable lives.

Mary Elizabeth Mahnkey was practical, optimistic and good-natured. She told of her life in a straight-forward, simple manner — sometimes funny, sometimes melancholy. One of her short poems may give a glimpse into her own life and how she viewed her hill county home.

Service
When they put away my silken scarf
My beads and thin worn rings,
Will they think of my old washtub
My broom and other things?
The little hoe I kept for flowers
The basket for dead leaves--
No one will use them any more
And so my spirit grieves. [119]

Ellen Gray Massey says in her inspiring biography of Mahnkey, "Writing with understanding for and about Ozark men, women, and children, she dispelled the hillbilly caricature of their culture and allowed readers to see its dignity and value." [120]

Today, Oasis lies over one hundred feet beneath the clear water of Table Rock Lake. But the stories of Mary Mahnkey live on, a testament to the strength and fortitude of the Ozark hillfolk. [121]

*Mary Elizabeth Mahnkey*

In his winsome autobiography, Douglas Mahnkey, son of Mary Elizabeth Mahnkey, tells a story that illustrates the hillsman's ability as a smart trader. [122]

"Uncle Wilse took off his big black hat and squinted his eyes very knowingly as he related this experience.

'One day some years ago, me and Aunt Sally was a-settin' on our front porch, and I looked up the road and there I seed a feller a-comin' horseback and leadin' a string of about twenty horses and ponies. He rid up and I asked him to get off his horse and set a spell, which he did, and had a good cold drink from our well. Then he began to blow about what he was goin' to do. He said, 'You see that string of horses there; well, I am goin' down into Arkansas in them mountains and get rich tradin' with them hillbillies.' This feller was from Kansas and shore didn't know much about our people.'

'Well, I didn't say nothin', just let him blow and brag 'til he got tired and bade us goodbye and was off to Arkansas to get rich tradin' with the hillbillies. Well, about six weeks later, me and Aunt Sally was settin' on our front porch. And I looked down the Narrows road to the south and I seed this same feller a-comin', afoot. He walked like he was all done in, and I asked him to come and set a spell with us on the porch, and I drew a fresh bucket of that good well water, and he drank good and long. He didn't say much, and finally I sez to him, sez I, 'How did you make out tradin' with them hillbillies? I don't see no stock.' And the man from Kansas said, 'I am busted, flat busted. Them hillbillies are ignorant, as ignorant as hell, but by God it won't do to trade with 'em.'"

In the preface to his autobiography, Douglas Mahnkey, who would serve as a State Representative and Taney County Prosecuting Attorney and in a private law practice that spanned six decades, reflects on the source of strength for his beloved mountain people:

"Sometimes in this modern day we wonder in amazement at the energy and fortitude of these people, our grandsires. They endured winter's cold and summer's drought; they knew sickness with no doctor at hand; they faced Indians, outlaws and famine with the same resolute courage. What philosophy, what logic enabled them to bear all those burdens and hardships through those dark days? We know they did survive and carve out for themselves and their children a way of life in these Ozarks that has become the envy of this modern, rushing generation. Their great-grandchildren have built the country our visitors now see as they travel the highways through these hills."

"Out of it all has come the conclusion that the Ozarks pioneers had a deep religious conviction, a strong will, a strong sense of justice, a willingness to endure hardship, an ability to make the best of any situation, a sense of humor, a ready wit, a quick answer, a bent for fun, a sharp intuition and a love for the hills and streams which they had chosen for home." [123]

At the turn of the century, Leon Weaver left his family's farm near Ozark, Missouri and joined a travelling medicine show. Raised in a musical family, Leon had learned to play several home-made musical instruments, including the musical saw. Leon's brother Frank joined the troupe and the Weaver brothers refined their entertainment chops as they traveled the country.

In 1921, the pair formed their own vaudeville act, the Arkansas Travelers (sometimes billed as the R-Can-Saw Travellers), added Leon's wife June and began touring as the Weaver Brothers and Elviry. Their combination of music, dancing, and homespun humor was well received. The group played large venues across America, toured Europe and even had a performance for the Queen of England. They were a frequent act on the *Grand Ole Opry*.

Leon and Elviry divorced in 1930. Despite Elviry's subsequent marriage to Frank, the group stayed together and continued their tight, clever "hillbilly" show. They performed on radio shows throughout the Depression years and in 1938 entered the movie business with *Swing Your Lady* (with Humphrey Bogart in the cast). Multiple movies followed including *Down in Arkansaw*, *Jeepers Creepers* with Roy Rogers, *Grand Ole Opry* with Roy Acuff, *In Old Missouri*, and *Shepherd of the Ozarks*.

The Weaver Brothers and Elviry found a performance style that appealed to a mass audience. Though by no means considered "high art", their combination of musical ability, stage presence and lowbrow humor was well received. They represented another dichotomous view of the hillbilly that sold nicely.

The Weaver Brothers were clearly talented. Their songs and dances were simple, but capably performed. Their humor was silly, but contained elements of mountain intelligence and common sense. Their costumes were typical rustic outfits, but were colorful and appropriate for the style they espoused. Elviry's stage dress was often purposely tacky and her portrayals sometimes shrewish.

The Weaver Brothers and Elviry fell back on many of the hackneyed depictions of the hillbilly, but they did it in a friendly manner. They played roles that were commercially liked and to some degree even admired. They deserve some credit for portraying at least a capable persona of mountain folk, but they also contributed to the old stereotyped perceptions of silliness and coarseness.

The Weaver Brothers and Elviry's movie career lasted well into the 1940s. These were definitely B movies and their film appearances lacked the crisp pace of their live show. They were part of a Hollywood vogue that produced a slew of sloppy, low budget hillbilly films. These movies played a significant role in advancing negative stereotypes of the Ozarks mountain people.
124

***The Weaver Brothers and Elviry***

The American movie industry had latched on to "hillbilly" themes in the very early 1900s. Nickelodeon shorts like *The Moonshiner* and *A Kentucky Feud* set the tone as early as 1904.

Urban dwellers ate up these melodramas of rural people. In his book *Hillbillyland*, J.W. Williamson says that at least seventy-one films were released in 1914 exploiting hillbilly stereotypes. [125]

These early films promulgated all the negative stereotypes of hillfolk. The first use of the term "hillbilly" was in the 1915 silent film *Billie — the Hill Bill*, a typical "city boy rescues mountain lass" insult. [126] By the 1920s, pictures were expanding their negative treatment of "them mountain folk" with comical characters. These portrayals may have been somewhat less threatening, but they certainly did not provide any rectification to the damaging image of the highland folk the movies loved to lampoon.

The farcical depictions of rural characters had a substantial history to stand on. Marcus Byrn's David Rattlehead, Noland's Pete Whetstone, and Thorpe's Jim Doggett set a precedent for the creation of a comical mountain dwelling persona. Films, radio and music all capitalized on the popularity of making fun of the Ozarks bumpkin. Ozarkers themselves were not averse to playing these roles and collecting audiences and ticket revenues for the farcical portrayals.

After years of working the vaudeville circuit, Bob Burns of Van Buren, Arkansas hit the bigtime as a hillbilly comic on New York and Los Angeles radio in the 1930s. Burns also plied the film business working in several movies over his career. He had a popular comedy and music radio program *The Arkansas Traveler* that aired from 1941 to 1947.

But Burns was no fool. He was known for creating unusual musical instruments from common materials, including the "bazooka", fashioned originally from a gas pipe. The "bazooka" would become a namesake for the effective World War II anti-tank weapon.

Bob Burns became a wealthy man, in no small part due to his savvy portrayals of comic rustics. His characters combined silliness with a measure of country intellect that was popular with both urban and rural consumers. [127]

***Bob Burns with his "bazooka"***

The hillbilly comedian was a very popular figure between the first and second World Wars. In addition to the Weaver Brothers and Bob Burns, performers like Lum and Abner and Will Rogers held a large audience and contributed to the dichotomous view of country folk and the mountain highlander in particular.

Spurred by these successful personalities, new outlandish characters were developed in animation. Walter Lantz' *Hill Billys* was released in 1935 followed by Warner Brothers' *When I Yoo Hoo*, *A Feud There Was*, *Naughty Neighbors* (with Porky and Petunia Pig), and *Musical Mountaineers* (starring Betty

Boop). [128] Freed somewhat by the art form, animation could run wild with the boorish images of the hillbilly. In fairness, everyone was fair game in these cartoons. The "urban idiot" was often lampooned equally.

In 1934, Paul Webb's *The Mountain Boys* (single panel cartoons), Billy DeBeck's Snuffy Smith (in the *Barnie Google and Snuffy Smith* comic strip) and Al Capp's *Li'l Abner* (comic strips) debuted. Webb's cartoons ran in *Esquire* magazine for several years and contributed to the crude image of shiftless, long-bearded, shoeless, ignorant mountain dwellers. [129]

As a central character in *Barney Google and Snuffy Smith*, Snuffy Smith has represented a stereotypical mountaineer for over eighty-five years. DeBeck's hillbilly characterizations do not reveal anything new. Their appearance and behaviors are the tried and true aphorisms of negative presentations. Snuffy does show some traits of independence and rugged mountain skills, but these only partially offset the typical worn out images.

Over its long run (1934 to 1977), the *Li'l Abner* comic strip probably achieved more notice for the farcical hillbilly persona than any other. Originally centered in Kentucky, *Li'l Abner's* hometown Dogpatch has become decidedly associated with the Arkansas Ozarks, particularly after the Dogpatch USA theme park opened in Newton County in 1968.

Al Capp spared no insult in his characterizations of the residents of Dogpatch. The main characters, the Yocum family consisting of Mammy, Pappy and Little Abner along with Daisy Mae (nee Scragg and eventually Abner's bride), bore all the typical traits of mountain rubes. Capp's comic strip expanded its cast to include scores of absurd players creating a world of opportunities to tease and denigrate rural lifestyles. *Li'l Abner* included some recognition of positive hill folk qualities such as honesty and common sense, but the overriding impact is one of ridicule and condescension.

But Capp liked to spread his satire around. He criticized urbanites, intellectual elites and capitalists right alongside the Yocums. His thinly veiled political criticisms and social commentary morphed over the decades and his personal life was eventually rocked by scandal.

*Li'l Abner* spawned plays, movies, musicals and comic strip imitations. These offspring rarely held the complexity or breadth of commentary that Capp created. They merely piggybacked on the world that was Dogpatch. Little Abner existed in an alternate universe that was at some level wholesome and good-natured, but was ultimately mean-spirited and derogatory. [130]

The twenty-year period between the two World Wars saw massive changes in media, culture, economic conditions and class distinctions. All these factors impacted the image and view of the "hillbilly". With the advent of radio, talking movies and the associated explosion of commercial music, the treatment of rural people and particularly mountain rurals, was exposed, exploited and manipulated.

These treatments often took the same track of relying on stereotyped images and characterizations. The hillfolk were yoked with moonshining, feuding, laziness, promiscuity, violence, inbreeding, poor hygiene, idiocy, and immorality. Granted, depictions were often mollified by bestowing elements of humor, individualism, hardiness and even shrewdness. But the general representation was negative.

The picture of the hillbilly presented to the world by commercial media was a continuation of a construct developed and perpetuated much earlier by outland chroniclers and humorists. There was an alternate positive sentiment that did deserve and did receive some notice. The art of people like May Kennedy McCord and Mary Elizabeth Mahnkey presented a more accurate and much more pleasant mountain image. Historians and folklorists like Vance Randolph and Otto Rayburn brought their first-hand experiences to a fairly significant audience. And the actual stories of folk like Vineta Wingate and Sanford Garland are a testament to the productive and admirable lives that have been carved out of these hills and hollows.

The creation of folk festivals throughout the Ozarks established a means to discover, salvage and perpetuate art forms, skills and cultural attributes that were quickly dying out. The music business created a whole new audience for mountain music and started trends that would lead to the preservation of some forms while begetting entirely novel genres.

The Great Depression brought national attention to the plight of the poor and shone a light on the disparate living conditions in rural America. The evils of the Depression resulted in programs that did in some cases improve the lives of poor Ozarkers, but at the same time contributed to mass migration out of the hills and the dwindling of many of the old mountain ways.

Americans at large were not quite sure what to do with the Ozarks hillbilly — laugh at him, sympathize with him, respect him or despise him. Some saw the mountain folk as a dying breed of frontier individualists who no longer played an important role in the future of the country. Others saw him as an antiquity that should be studied and preserved before he disappeared. Others saw him as the example of a pure-bred American standard (i.e. white, Anglo-Saxon, protestant) that should be glorified and nurtured. A few saw the mountain folk as just another cultural subset with their own belief systems, positive attributes and foibles.

The upheavals of the period between the wars would forever change all Americans and have a permanent impact on the actual and perceived image of the Ozarks mountain people. After World War II, the rural folk of southern Missouri and northern Arkansas would begin to be more fully absorbed into the typical American lifestyle. Some of the old ways still remained in the more isolated outposts, but it would become harder and harder for the mountain culture to avoid the creep of modernization.

During the first half of the twentieth century, all forms of media contributed to a nationally perceived image of country folk. This image was typically applied to the people of the Appalachia and Ozarks regions, but also began to be applied to poor folk in other areas — the South in general, displaced mid-western tenant farmers, the poor laboring class moving into the industrial cities, and the migrant farm workers, both domestic and foreign, who followed the harvest seasons across the country.

Through magazine and newspaper articles, novels, plays, music shows, radio, and movies, the portrayals of the hillbilly tropes were ingrained in the national consciousness. Some forms were kinder than others. But particularly in the poorly researched and condescending newspaper and movie depictions, the images used were often negative and did not represent the positive attributes of mountain folk.

Tourists came to the Ozarks to enjoy the scenery, the hunting and fishing, the beautiful lakes and streams, and the peace and solitude. But many of them came expecting to see a "real hillbilly". They had preconceived ideas of what a hillbilly looked like and how they acted. Local folks were often insulted by these gawkers and the boosters made efforts to dispel these images. But some Ozarkers saw the silly representations as a commercial opportunity and they did take advantage of it.

# Chapter 5

## Competing Hillbilly Images

*Ermal Phillips* straddled the barbed wire fence and hiked his other leg over the strand. He walked through the brush toward a copse of small trees and pointed out the crumbling remains of the root cellar. "This was used for storage of vegetables and also as a storm shelter," Ermal explained. Just beyond the cellar were the collapsed remains of a rock well. Ermal described how the hand-dug well had a small roof over it that supported a bucket on a rope and pulley.

"The house was over here. It was a nice house with a porch on three sides." All that could be seen now were the footing for the large central fireplace, part of a concrete foundation wall and scattered red bricks. The home of Ermal's grandfather, Anderson Phillips, had burned many years ago. Now the homesite, crowded with fast growing sumac trees, was hidden between the expansive pastures of Hickum Prairie and the rocky, wooded hillsides tapering down to the headwaters of Sweetwater Creek. Ermal collected two broken bricks. "For our rock garden," he explained.

Back out on the county road, about two miles north of Golden, Ermal indicated the house he grew up in. The original log house has been remodeled and covered with siding. "This was our family farm on forty acres. We leased other property to grow crops. We kept our dairy cows here — Guernseys, Jerseys and Brown Swiss. We always milked by hand. Our family never had electricity in any place we lived until we left Missouri and moved to Idaho in 1947."

A little north of Ermal's boyhood home is the school he first attended, Carter. The school was named for the Carter family who donated an acre of land for the building. Eventually, the stub of land between the lower Kings River and the White River became known as the Carter area. The school is gone now. Donated to the Kanakuk Kamp, the building burned before it could be moved. Only a quiet acre of land exists now where the school bell once rang.

Ermal lived at the old homeplace with his parents Elvin and Nettie (Davis) Phillips and his two brothers and two sisters. Everyone helped on the farm. While Elvin worked the fields and the livestock, Nettie tended the vegetable garden, took care of the chickens and separated the cream. After removing the cream with a hand separator, Nettie would feed the milk whey to the hogs. Sometimes she would press the curd and whey in a cheesecloth and produce a homemade cheese, similar to the consistency of cottage cheese. The row crops the Phillips grew were primarily fed to their livestock. Eggs and cream were sold at the Cope or Weddington store in Golden.

In the 1930s, Golden, Missouri had a post office, two general stores run by Bud Cope and T.H. Weddington, and the Baptist Church. In 1938, the rock schoolhouse was built in Golden as a WPA (Works Projects Administration) project. Elvin Phillips worked as a timekeeper on the Federal government sponsored building. The school served the area for many years as an elementary and two-year high school and is now a library and community building.

In 1938, Ermal's family moved to the Jakie Spring area to farm and be near Nettie's family, the Davises. They also continued to farm property in the Carter area. Jakie Spring is a year-round, free-flowing spring about one mile southeast of Golden. It is part of the source for Jakie Creek and is named for Jacob Lemaster, an early settler in the area and maternal great-grandfather of Ermal Phillips.

Ermal Phillips' family worked the land at Jakie Spring. Ermal tells of plowing the fields behind their mules when he was considered old enough at nine years of age.

"I wasn't strong enough to swing the plow around when we'd come to the end. I'd have to circle the team at the end, run them back in and get them lined up with the furrow. Then I'd lift up the plow and get it back in the ground. One time, I threw a fit 'cause I couldn't get the plow turned around. Mom got a kick oughta that."

"We planted sorghum cane for molasses. We had a molasses mill down by the spring. We stripped the leaves and seed heads off the stalks. We put the stalks through the mill. The mill was operated by our mule, Maude. Maude was hitched to a long pole. She walked 'round and 'round to run the mill. The juice ran out of the mill down a trough to a big divided vat. We had a fire under the vat to cook down the juice. We skimmed off the top and the molasses settled in the bottom. We put it in fruit jars. We gave some away and used it at home."

Ermal and his brothers also hunted squirrels and rabbits and trapped skunk, possum, mink and muskrat in steel traps. "There was a good market for pelts. I remember my uncle Frank Davis trapped wolves and coyotes for their furs. I didn't like the trapping, I'm kind-hearted. But it was for survival," Ermal reminisces.

"Sweetwater was where they found 'Old Bill.' Old Bill was a family horse that was found dead in the creek. I was about four years old, but remember Dad taking a team and dragging our beloved old work horse across the field to a far corner and leavin' him there for the buzzards and coyotes to eat. When I passed the carcass, it made me sick, but I seldom had to pass by. That sight of Old Bill's dry bones layin' out there in that open field still haunts me today."

From their place at Jakie, the Phillips could travel by horse or wagon up to Golden and then on the gravel 39 Highway north to the White River. Old Highway 39 roughly followed Viney Creek down past Rube Dick's store, down to the river bottom, across the White River on the Golden Bridge built in 1929, and on to Mano. Ermal says his uncle Frank Davis operated the ferry at Golden for a time.

Ermal's brother Raymond was killed in a tragic automobile accident out on old Highway 39 in 1943. The Phillips family moved to Exeter in 1944 so Ermal could attend high school there. Ermal's father relocated his family to Idaho in 1947.

Ermal never lost his connection to the land on Hickum Prairie. In 1998, Ermal and his wife Verla Mae (Cole) purchased the land surrounding Jakie Spring. They built an attractive, country style home on the swath just above the spring named for Ermal's ancestor. Ermal protected the spring and the land around it. He appreciated the life-giving force of this soil, this water. He passed this reverence for the land on to his own children.[131]

Wilma (Rice) England was born in 1913 and grew up on a substantial farm on Mill Creek just east of Viola. Wilma's parents Derward (D.H.) and Della (Schreiner) Rice owned the property along Mill Creek where it ran into the White River. Wilma's grandfather William Henry Schreiner ran the Schreiner Ferry at Shell Knob.

William Washington Rice emigrated from Kentucky in the late 1800s when his son D.H. was two years old. William built a dog-trot style log cabin above Mill Creek. The house consisted of two large individual rooms connected by a passageway. Shortly after the log house was constructed, a two-room frame structure was added at the back, creating an L-shaped home with a dining room and kitchen. D.H. increased the Rice farmland and developed the family business. With three daughters and no sons, Derward often hired help for major farm work. He employed contract crews to thresh and bale hay, cut cordwood and shear sheep.

Wilma's childhood home did not have electricity until about 1949. They used kerosene Aladdin lamps for light. Cooking was done on a wood stove and later, a kerosene stove. With water drawn by hand from the well, laundry was done using a washtub and washboard. White laundry was boiled in a large cast iron kettle placed on top of the wood stove.

Wilma tended the chickens, helped with household chores and went to grade school at Hideout. She says the school took this name because "it was a little hard to find". As children, Wilma and her younger sister Mabel made the Rice farm their playground.

"My sister and I had playhouses all over the farm. Any field that my Dad would be working in, we'd build a playhouse on the edge of that field. When he moved on, we moved on, too. Our dog Fritz was often our companion."

Near the mouth of Mill Creek, there was a bluff shelter that the Rice family visited. Wilma says, "That shelter was our favorite spot. We'd go down and have lunch under there. We had no idea we were treading on graves. My mother would go down and build a fire while my father was working. We would have a picnic."

As part of the Table Rock Salvage Project, this bluff shelter was excavated in 1952-53 as a Native American archaeological site and named the Rice Shelter. The Rice Site was an attractive shelter for Native Americans. It had a fairly large (about 400 square feet) covered area and faced southeast, providing warmth from the sun and protection from north winds. There was a nearby spring, but the shelter itself remained dry.

Based on the type and style of artifacts excavated at Rice, three distinct cultural complexes were found to have inhabited the shelter —- an Early, Middle and Late. These complexes correspond to the Archaic through Mississippian Periods indicating the shelter could have been used up to 9,000 years ago.

Many shaped tools were unearthed at the Rice site including projectile points, scrapers, knives, manos, grinding stones and drills. One specific shaped projectile point found in the area was named the Rice Lobed. Other relics included shaped antlers, shell beads, stone pipes and bone punches. Pottery shards were discovered, particularly in the upper levels of the dig. Evidence of pottery, some decorated, included sand-, grit- and shell-tempered forms.

The excavation at the Rice Site uncovered seven human burials. The graves revealed a variety of remains from just a few fragments to an almost complete skeleton. Two of the graves included stones placed over the body. Some of the burials appeared to include offerings such as projectile points and a stone axe. One interment included the bones of a dog. [132]

The Rices grew corn, hay, oats and wheat and ran cattle and sheep on their farm. The mostly cleared farm was fenced and cross-fenced to create pasture and cropland and to separate the cattle from the sheep. There was a large vegetable garden. The livestock were regularly sold at market in Springfield. Much of the farm labor was done with the help of draft horses. D.H. finally bought a tractor in the 1940's. Wilma says, "He thought he should have the biggest tractor made. So he bought this huge one. The thing was so big, I could barely reach the brake pedal."

Prior to 1927, the Rice's could cross the White River on the Schreiner Ferry to go to Shell Knob and Cassville. But they most often visited Viola, only a half mile from their home. Wilma's uncle ran the McKee Mill. Viola had a general store that supplied staples, fabric, work shoes and farm supplies. Many items had to be purchased through mail order. Wilma says, "We did a lot of shopping from catalogs — Montgomery Ward, National Cloak and Suit Co., Sears and Roebuck, Chicago Mail Order. That's how we bought our clothes. We didn't get much like that at the local store."

There was a blacksmith shop in Viola for livery and farrier work and of course, the Christian and Baptist churches. Most rural churches of this era could not afford a full-time preacher. They relied on traveling preachers who would visit every month or so. On the other Sundays, the congregation would hold their own Sunday School.

Wilma recalls that her father spoke of a Viola town band that existed before she was born. Wilma also remembers, as a child and young woman, watching the Viola baseball team play ball. When asked if the girls ever played baseball, Wilma quips, "I remember my older sister Ella batting balls in high heels."

The Rice's neighbors included the Underwoods and the Hoods. Wilma's mother Della held quilting bees. Women would bring pieced tops and stretch them on a large quilting rack Della had at their home. The ladies would work together to quilt the top to the backing. They would sometimes make a friendship quilt with each person supplying a signed and dated square. There were music parties with musicians and singing and square dances held in people's homes.

Wilma Rice attended a two-year high school in Shell Knob. It was common at the time for young people to move to town and board with someone while attending high school. They would spend weekdays at school and return to the farm for the weekend. Wilma finished high school in Blue Eye.

After high school, Wilma married George England. George worked for the U.S. Forest Service and then as a civilian for the U.S. Army at Malden Air Base in southeast Missouri. George moved his family to California in 1946. In 1959, as Table Rock Lake began to cover parts of the Rice property, D.H. and Della sold their farm and moved to Berryville. With their advancing age, the large farm had become too difficult for D.H. to maintain. Wilma says, "My father was a good farmer and manager. My mother was a good manager and housekeeper. It makes me sad to go there now. I remember how it used to be. That was a pretty farm."

Wilma's daughter Ann (England) King spent some time on the Rice farm as a child. She reminisces:

"I was heartbroken when my family left here. I did not want to go to California. I hated leaving my grandmother. I loved it on the farm. I loved the look and smell of the kerosene lamps. I felt very safe there. My grandparents could do or handle anything. I loved the farm. Sometimes we'd walk down to White River. I would wade in the river. I loved to go for a wagon ride."

When much of the Rice farm was buried by Table Rock Lake in 1959, Mill Creek changed from a flowing brook to a large lake cove over a quarter mile wide. The Rice Shelter and the secrets it held were forever lost beneath the lake. [133]

Ermal Phillips and Wilma Rice were no bumpkins. They lived a good life growing up on small farms in the Ozarks. They became successful adults with fond memories of their life in the hills and their tough, but honest upbringing. They epitomize the type of people who grew up in and of this land.

*Wilma (Rice) England at the Rice farm 1940*

Following World War II, Americans jumped aboard an expanding economy, embraced modernization and took advantage of increased mobility and better communications. The Ozarks joined this era of prosperity, too, particularly the towns and cities of the region. Isolation from broader society became more and more rare.

The continuation of a Spartan, backwoods existence was becoming almost impossible. With rural electrification, school consolidation, the impracticalities of the small family farm, demographic shifts to the cities, and even the introduction of tele-vision, an old mountain way of life was passing away. Even if one desired to stay in a more sheltered, non-urban environment, it was nearly impossible to avoid the influences of a quickly changing, more homogenous society.

Portrayals of country folk in the entertainment business followed the same general trend they had been on for decades. Some were downright awful like *Maid in the Ozarks*, some were positive like Wilson Rawls *Where the Red Fern Grows*, but most stayed with the farcical or comic presentations like *Li'l Abner* and *Ma and Pa Kettle*.

In the music business, the "hillbilly" genre was being ab-sorbed into wider, more "professional" categories like bluegrass, folk and country. Music promoters and publishers eschewed the "hillbilly" moniker, but continued to recognize the talent and value of the mountain musicians and their songs. The inclusion of the "hillbilly" fool remained a common theme in commercial-ized mountain music programs.

It is difficult to find a similar example of so much direct use of humor associated with any other form of music. Perhaps Victor Borge in the classical realm or Spike Jones and Steve Allen in the popular fields are comparable, but they were basi-cally making fun of the music and not presenting themselves as a separate comic character.

What is it about mountain music that almost seems to require the addition of the fool? Does this allow the listener to atone for some guilt for liking this music? Does it allow the performer to acknowledge that they realize this is not "real" music? Does it allow the audience to assuage their enjoyment of "low art" with the excuse that "well, it's really just comedy"?

If musicians, promoters and listeners of hillbilly music were embarrassed, they did not seem to mind. Country music shows continued to be very popular on radio, on the stage and even-tually on television. The compositions had moved a long ways away from the original old English and Celtic ballads, but the basic simple melodies, musical structure and lyrics retained an admiring following.

Hollywood continued to promote a twisted view of the hill people. Maybe the screen productions sold tickets, but they certainly did not offer an honest view of Ozarks life. If you spend some time in the Ozarks, you will find poor people, you will find people with minimal education, and you will find people prone to criminal behavior, just like everywhere else. Too many outlanders, too many script writers, and too many news reporters have chosen to portray the stereotypes. Perhaps if one chose to "sit a spell" and listen, a more balanced view would be revealed.

It is difficult to find a movie production that gives a fair shrift to the mountain dweller. One would presume that *The Shepherd of the Hills* would be a good starting point. The 1919 silent version would be expected to be true to the original romantic novel as it was directed by Harold Bell Wright. However, the film is presumed lost, so one can only guess at its character treatment.

Another silent version was produced in 1928, apparently fairly true to Wright's story. The 1941 adaptation was another matter. Starring John Wayne, the movie contains some panoramic non-Ozark mountain scenes. But the script was substantially modified and hillbilly cliches crept in, ruining the intent of Wright's novel. A fourth *Shepherd of the Hills* filmed in Branson was released in 1964. Although employing some local talent, this version's script was also rewritten and missed the point of the original story.

From its very early days, the movie industry chose to portray mountain folk as backwards, illiterate, and dangerous, feuding hicks. Many of these B flicks pandered to the perceptions of vulgar and promiscuous mountain folk. By the 1920s and 30s, a spate of comedic hillbilly films had been released to the viewing public. Often based on popular musical and radio "country" personalities like the Weaver Brothers and Elviry, Lum and Abner, and Bob Burns, these movies were cranked out in droves, usually relying on the same old banalities of country life with the addition of watered down hillbilly music.

Not to be outdone, the play *Maid in the Ozarks* was first staged in Los Angeles in 1940. Often cited as "the worst play in the world", the production was very popular, touring the country for years. The premise of the script is irrelevant. *Maid* relied on awful depictions of Ozarks people using sexual references, scatological humor and idiotic characters. [134] In the 1950s, Jack Nicholson played a leading role in a production of the farce — certainly a part he avoided on his resume. [135]

*Maid in the Ozarks playbill*

The Ma and Pa Kettle characters were first introduced in Betty MacDonald's popular, but somewhat insulting book *The Egg and I* in 1945. Although not connected to the Ozarks directly, MacDonald's Kettles were silly, but kindhearted bumpkins. Universal Studios translated the Kettles into a comic and supposedly endearing couple in the 1947 cinematic *The Egg and I*, with Marjorie Main and Percy Kilbride as the Kettles and Fred MacMurray and Claudette Colbert as the naïve city slickers. [136]

Ma and Pa Kettle were featured in a series of their own movies from 1949 to 1957. Following Kilbride's death, *The Kettles in the Ozarks* replaced Pa's character with his brother played by Arthur Honnicutt who owns a backwoods farm in Arkansas.

The movie-going public seemed to enjoy the comic presentation of the Kettles as hillbillies who fumbled around their farmstead populated with multiple children, constantly encountering problems with urbanites, capitalists and big city shysters. Despite their apparent innocence and gullibility, the Kettles always managed to win out over their antagonists.

One actor who represented the hillbilly throughout much of his career was Andy Griffith. Many of Griffith's roles were characterized by dichotomous traits of the hillbilly. His portrayals sometimes relayed the simple-minded stereotype of the mountain man, but they also contained elements that were endearing and even praiseworthy. In his 1957 film debut, Griffith starred in *A Face in the Crowd*. It is a complex role that introduces him as a simple, folksy musician. Groomed by his big city mentor, he becomes a popular radio personality and pitchman who moves into television.

Andy's character, Larry Rhodes, becomes involved in politics and slowly his negative traits are revealed and developed as he is consumed by fame and his own ego. Eventually, Rhodes' supporters turn on him and he is left bemoaning his own downfall. *A Face in the Crowd* relies on some of the bromides of country personality, but it does treat Griffith's character with a much wider range of human qualities.

Griffith translated his country boy image into several successful roles in movies and television. In *No Time for Sergeants* and *Onionhead* he plays a bumbling, but likeable country rube. These roles were less complex than the *Face in the Crowd* character. They helped establish Griffith as a generally positive model for the simple, generous hillsman.

Andy Griffith achieved considerable fame in the 1960s as the good natured, wise Sheriff Taylor on television's eight seasons of *The Andy Griffith Show*. Sheriff Taylor did a good job of providing an example of positive rural traits. He was calm, thoughtful and imbued with common sense. His relationship with his son Opie and aunt Bee were loving and protective.

*The Andy Griffith Show* played off frequent interactions between Andy, his bumbling deputy Barney Fife, and a gaggle of generally comic townspeople in the show setting of Mayberry.

Attuned to a long-standing tradition, the show often revolved around Sheriff Taylor outsmarting outsiders or smoothing over town rivalries.

Although Griffith's Mayberry character was almost always portrayed in a positive light, many of the other roles and plot lines tended to rely on stereotypes. Several of the supporting characters were consistently foolish or comic. When "hillbillies" like Ernest T. Bass or the Darlings were included in the script, these characters combined comic elements with an ignorant, almost menacing persona. They were presented as "outsiders" to the town residents, i.e. the town elites.

Mountain music was an occasional part of the show with Griffith providing pleasant ballad-like performances and the Darlings, played by the Dillards, performing adept bluegrass.

The characters Andy Griffith portrayed over his long career in movies, television and recording present a fairly positive image of the rural male. Although more associated with Appalachia than the Ozarks, Griffith established a post-war interpretation of rural characters and settings that held both constructive and detrimental facets. Sometimes his roles can be viewed as exhibiting intelligence, kindness, and competence. In other portrayals, his characters were silly, bumbling, or ignorant. Griffith played all these roles well. How his viewers interpreted these depictions is probably a result of their background, heritage and region of origin.

Throughout its very popular radio shows, live performances and television broadcasts, the *Grand Ole Opry* has presented a professional image of country music for almost one hundred years. The *Opry* has generally eschewed the moniker "hillbilly", but in more recent years, some of its performers have embraced the title.

The long-running concert series has expanded from its early promotion of old-time music to include western, bluegrass, gospel, popular and the broad category of "country" music. Dancing and comedy have been a part of the *Opry* from its early days including performers like The Weaver Brothers and Elviry and Minnie Pearl.

Minnie Pearl (Sarah Ophelia Colley Cannon) provided wry comedy on the *Opry* for more than fifty years and continued her role on television's *Hee Haw* from 1969 to 1991. Her sketches were often self-deprecating and mildly made fun of her "hillbilly" background (she was actually from a prosperous family and a college graduate).

In *Hillybillyland*, J.W. Williamson notes that the hillbilly image was initially eschewed by Nashville's business community. But as country music grew in importance, they embraced the monetary potential of both the serious and comedic elements of "hillbilly" music.[137]

Despite the *Opry* founder George D. Hay's dismissal of the hillbilly epithet (see p. 152), country folk (at least of the commercial country music scene), have often welcomed the description. [138]

Dolly Parton, one of the best-known and best-loved country singers captured the duality of the term's use well, commenting that in the music business, the term can be a source of pride, but depending on the context, almost a racist remark. [139]

The Ozarks received national attention through broadcasts of the *Ozark Jubilee* from 1954 to 1960. Produced out of Springfield, the *Jubilee* originated as a radio show, Korn's-a-Krackin', recorded before a live audience. Drawing on a vast supply of local talent and adding nationally known country music stars, the production expanded to a weekly television show and became very popular.

The *Jubilee* was a quick paced production with lots of music, square dancing and some comedy. Hosted by Red Foley, the *Ozark Jubilee* presented a downhome depiction that was well accepted by large portions of the American audience. The show had a clean-cut image. Soft-spoken emcees and entertainers, well-dressed and personable, belied the rough hillbilly image often portrayed in contemporary movies and literature. The comedy routines were silly, but generally avoided the offensive mountain folk caricatures that had riddled much of the entertainment media.

The *Ozark Jubilee* hosted a multitude of country music stars — so many that listing them seems futile. Suffice it to say that over its long run, the show featured just about every well-known country music entertainer of the time. Additionally, the *Jubilee* helped catapult the careers of many musicians including Brenda Lee, Porter Waggoner, Pat Boone and Grandpa Jones.

The Ozarks needed a positive presentation of its people and their talents. The *Ozark Jubilee* did an admirable job of presenting the region and its culture to the wider American scene. [140]

The Ozarks has been irreversibly altered by the construction of several large lake impoundments. The first major dam on the White River, Powersite, created Lake Taneycomo in 1913. The 22-mile long lake became a significant tourist attraction and led to the further development of Branson as a vacation destination. With the White River Railroad completed through Branson by 1904, access to the Ozarks hill country along the White River improved considerably.

The float fishing business thrived during the first half of the 20th century. Floats on the rivers of southern Missouri and northern Arkansas were very popular with a wealthy clientele from the big Midwestern cities. Camps sprung up all along these rivers, providing long-term vacation stays for entire families. But the building of the big dams eventually diminished much of the float business.

*Vacationers at Camp Clark Galena (around 1914)*

Bagnell Dam impounded the Osage in 1931, followed by Bull Shoals in 1951, Table Rock in 1959 and Beaver in 1965, all on the White. Big dams created Lake Wappapello on the St. Francis in 1941, Lake Norfork on the North Fork River in 1944 and Greers Ferry on the Little Red River in 1963. Efforts by the Corps of Engineers to impound the Current and Jacks Fork were thwarted by the creation of the Ozark National Scenic Riverways and the Buffalo was saved when it was declared the first National River in 1972.

Although the float fishing business was hurt by dam construction, the lake impoundments created a whole new opportunity for outdoor recreation. The combination of large reservoirs and the remaining unimpounded, free flowing streams made for a vacation paradise in the Ozarks. When combined with the attraction of old-time music, arts and crafts, and a bucolic lifestyle, the Ozarks became a first rate destination for vacationers and retirement living.

Despite the frequent bashing they took from popular media, Ozarks folk knew they had something to offer. In addition to the natural wonders of rolling hills, forested valleys, clear flowing streams and the new lakes, Ozarkers possessed a culture rich in storytelling, skilled crafts, music and homeopathic medicine. The mountain people accepted these talents as part of their way of life and necessities for existence in a rugged environs.

Some outlanders and some local elites viewed the mountain culture as a dying, primitive lifestyle that no longer had a place in a modern society and reflected poorly on the region. Others saw these attributes as valuable, unique qualities that were worthy of study and preservation.

In the first half of the twentieth century, serious documentation of the Ozarks culture was undertaken by researchers like Otto Rayburn and Vance Randolph, even as by their own admission, the region was changing quickly and losing its unique traits. Recording, photographing and writing down the facets of mountain life were important. But many saw the need to encourage and salvage the fast dwindling cultural elements of the Ozark Highlands. So rose the craft, music and folk festivals.

With plenty of star power, the Ozarkian Hillcrofters were responsible for some of the earliest festivals. But their efforts were limited and seemed to exist primarily as get-togethers for their members and friends. Starting in 1932, the Hillcrofters held semi-annual gatherings at various Ozarks locales: a spring meeting called the Feast of the Mayapple and a fall party, the Festival of Painted Leaves. [141] These affairs eventually drifted away, as did the Hillcrofters organization itself after a few years.

Although the Hillcrofters' festivals seemed to do little more than promote their ideals within their own ranks, they did provide a stepping stone for events with a broader reach. Supported by Randolph, Rayburn, and particularly May McCord, larger festivals were established and began to attract considerable regional and eventually national audiences. "The first folk festival in the Ozarks took place in the spring of 1934 at the Basin Park Hotel in Eureka Springs... Directing the program were May Kennedy McCord and Sam Leath, a Eureka Springs tour guide, Indian enthusiast, and chamber of commerce president." [142]

May McCord helped organize folk fairs across the Ozarks beginning in the mid-1930s. These events were often music talent shows attracting local musicians and singers. Held at regional towns like Mountain View and Eureka Springs in Arkansas and Branson and West Plains in Missouri, the winners of the local shows would advance to larger festivals held in Springfield and St. Louis.

In 1941, the Stone County (Arkansas) Folkways Festival was held in Mountain View at the Blanchard Springs Recreation Area featuring music and jig dancing contests. World War II ended a repeat of the festival, but it was revived in 1963 by the Ozark Foothills Handicraft Guild. These events would lead to the establishment of Mountain View as perhaps the best promoter of authentic Ozarks crafts and music.

In 1954, the first Ozarks Arts and Crafts Fair was held at War Eagle, Arkansas at the site of the historic War Eagle Mill. This event has continued each year as a fall festival and is recognized for its dedication to presenting and preserving traditional Ozarks arts and crafts.

The Ozark Folk Center in Mountain View has worked hard to maintain a commitment to genuine Ozarks cultural elements. Mountain View is truly representative of an interior, isolated mountain enclave. With no railroad and poor road access, Mountain View, Stone County's seat since 1873, remained far from outside influences for much of its existence. It's a beautiful region that has held fast to its pioneer heritage.

Mountain View, Arkansas must be congratulated for its efforts to recognize and preserve true mountain culture. Particularly when considering the awful exposure it received from an infamous event in 1929.

The story and court case based on the alleged murder of Connie Franklin and the alleged rape of his girlfriend Tiller Ruminer is well-told by Brooks Blevins in *Ghost of the Ozarks*. [143] Thoroughly researched and dramatically told, Blevins describes the events that occurred in and around small, isolated Mountain View against the perceived and actual culture of the Ozarks Highlands.

This crime story is convoluted and complicated. Briefly, it starts with a transient calling himself Connie Franklin courting a young, very poor mountain lass Tiller Ruminer who lives near St. James about fourteen miles east of Mountain View. They quickly decide to get married, but on a return walk from an unsuccessful visit to the local Justice of the Peace, they are waylaid by five men. The story that Tiller eventually relates to the local sheriff is that she was raped by two of the attackers while Connie was beaten, burned alive, dismembered and his remains dumped in a nearby creek.

After months of investigation, charges were brought against the five accused attackers and a trial was held in December of 1929. The sordid qualities of the alleged crimes attracted scores of reporters to the little county seat just south of the White River. Just prior to the trial's beginning, a man showed up claiming to be Connie Franklin. Whether he is or is not Tiller's beau receives extensive attention and plays a major role in the outcome of the trial. Ultimately, the accused are found not guilty of murder and the rape charges are later dropped.

The Connie Franklin/Tiller Ruminer saga contains many elements of the negative perceptions of the hillbilly image propagated in mass media. This case received national attention in late 1929 and the sordid details were sensationalized by the plethora of reporters who descended on the little Ozarks town during the cold December trial.

Elements of vigilantism, violent behavior, moonshining, inbreeding and crushing poverty were all exploited in the yellow press stories. Perhaps the most outlandish accounts were those that chose to blame the awful events on a so-called system of "mountain feudalism". William G Secrist, a reporter for the Kansas City Journal Post, arrived in Mountain View to cover the trial and proceeded to pen several sensationalized articles about the people and events surrounding the tawdry case.

Secrist wrote, "The Ozarks 'barons' have made peons of the poor and illiterate, after the fashion of iron fisted Mexican bandit leaders, whipping men, women and children to drive them to work on the barons' estates even committing murder to enforce their commands. It has been the practice of the creek bottom gang for years to mark the young girls of the hill people as their property, for whatever use they wanted." [144]

As in nearly all commentary on the Ozarks culture written by outlanders and chroniclers, there is a kernel of truth behind these wild claims. Certainly there were class distinctions in the

White River Hills, just as there is everywhere else. The town elites and the "haves" could often be accused of taking advantage of a community's poorer "have nots". Occurrences of "rural justice" and vigilantism are well documented in the Ozarks, as they are in almost all other regions of the country.

But to expand the Franklin/Ruminer episode into a general damning of Mountain View's citizenry and the Ozarks culture at large seems both limited and unfair. The bulk of the reporting that came out of this case only exacerbated the perceived ideas and images of rural Ozarkers. Some regional Arkansas newspapers attempted to challenge the sensational press releases, but for the most part, the damage was done.

Mountain View would move on from the bad press it received in 1929. It would find ways to capture and extol its people's positive traits and abilities. The town and the region would capitalize on these assets and present them to an audience that would learn to appreciate and value mountain culture.

Jimmy Driftwood was born James Corbitt Morris in 1907 in Stone County, Arkansas. He grew up in a musical family and playing his home-made guitar, wrote thousands of songs. Driftwood is perhaps best known for his penning of *The Battle of New Orleans*, but his accomplishments went well beyond this simple, jingoistic tune.

In his typical out-sized, anecdotal style, Driftwood relates elements of his upbringing:

"When I was a boy growing up in the Ozarks, we never heard the term "folk music', but we sure played a lot of it. My dad taught me my first tunes on the guitar, sitting on the porch those long summer evenings after work was done in the fields and the woods. We played a guitar my grandpa made from a fence rail and an old ox yoke. Wintertimes we would often huddle around the fireplace till bedtime, singin' and pickin'. Saturday nights several families often got together to sing songs like "Barbara Allen', 'Old Joe Clark' or 'Knoxville Girl' — ballads as old as the hills." [145]

Driftwood extolled the musical culture of his Stone County home and propagated interest in the traditional and folk music roots that flourished in and around the mountain enclaves of north central Arkansas. He received national acclaim for his musical abilities, performing at Carnegie Hall, the *Grand Ole Opry* and the *Ozark Jubilee*. Jimmy received several Grammy Awards.

Jimmy Driftwood helped found the Rackensack Folklore Society and along with the Ozark Foothills Handicraft Guild was instrumental in establishing the Arkansas Folk Festival when it was revived in Mountain View in 1963. Music shows were held at the Stone County Courthouse every Friday night by the Rackensacks, filled with authentic performances by Ozarks balladeers. Driftwood's interests went beyond music. Driftwood hoped to preserve Ozarks culture through education, demonstration and environmental protections. He could also be controversial and has been accused of excessive self-promotion and embellishment.[146]

The success of the Rackensack Society and the Arkansas Folk Festival led to the establishment of the Ozark Folk Center in 1973 as a State Park. Driftwood served as musical director at the Center until 1975 when he was removed over disagreements on incorporation and performance fees. With several members of the Rackensacks, Driftwood built the Jimmy Driftwood Barn and Folklore Hall of Fame in Mountain View, providing another venue for traditional music and crafts.

Using his fame and influence, Driftwood fought to protect the Buffalo River from being dammed and helped secure its designation as the first National River. He also aided in protecting Blanchard Springs Cavern under ownership of the U.S. Forest Service.

The Ozarks festivals have generally done a good job of presenting realistic examples of true Ozarks culture, but over time, commercialization and cooptation have crept into some of them. Particularly with the festivals directly associated with tourist attractions like Silver Dollar City and Dogpatch, the authenticity of art forms and handicrafts presented has suffered.

In the post-war period, the outright slandering of the Ozarks hillbilly waned a bit. The hillbilly images portrayed in mass media and even in the promotional material of Ozarks boosters generally took on a romantic or comic view. There were exceptions;

some depictions of mountain people were downright awful, to the point of being dangerous.

Cultural mores and attitudes tend to run in cycles; what is popular becomes outdated, what is frowned upon becomes the new fascination. So it was with the image of the hillbilly. From the 1950s to the 1970s, there was renewed interest in traditional music, particularly folk and mountain music. There was a revived interest in rural, simplistic living through the "back to the land" movement. And there was newfound appreciation for all things primitive or hand-made.

The Ozarks provided good examples for these trends. With the big, new reservoirs, state parks and music and crafts fairs, the Ozarks region attracted visitors by the thousands. Most came to enjoy the scenery and "quaintness" of the hills and valleys. Some came to stay. Many chose the area as a retirement destination. This influx resulted in the continuation of modernization for the region. So on one hand, the rediscovery of the Ozarks was an economic boon, providing some improvement to the lives of the mountain folk. On the other hand, it tended to commercialize the very attributes that it claimed as authentic and accelerated the "loss of the old ways".

# Chapter 6

## The Hillbilly in Modern America

*Bob Mabe* was born in 1930 and raised on a forty acre farm near Highlandville, Missouri, near the route of the Wilderness Road. He grew up in a family with eleven children during the Depression. The Mabes grew tomatoes, corn, cucumbers and cane for molasses. They kept hogs and work horses to pull a turning plow.

Music was a part of Bob's life from an early age. He heard his mother singing the old ballads, "The Burglar Beau" and "Silver Dagger". When Bob was six, his older sister insisted he sing with his brother Bill every day. The two boys learned to sing over fifty songs in a tight, sibling harmony.

On one occasion, the Mabe brothers were asked to sing at a local church. When asked by the preacher what song they would do, Bob told him, "You Got to Walk That Lonesome Valley". "Oh, no," the preacher responded, "you can't sing that." They went on to perform another tune. Bob thinks the preacher had mistakenly confused the song with "Lonesome Cowboy", a decidedly secular tune.

Bob also sang with May Kennedy McCord in Eureka Springs and for a while did a fifteen minute radio show on KWTO with his sister and uncle. Bob began playing music with three of his brothers, Bill, Jim and Lyle. Bob played a guitar purchased for him by auctioneer Earl Blansit. Brother Bill played a "biscuit boy", a Hawaiian-style Dobro. Jim played the washboard and Lyle the washtub bass.

Bob was working a full-time job during the day and playing music with his brothers at night and on weekends around Springfield and Branson. They called themselves The Baldknobbers, borrowing the name from the notorious Ozarks vigilante group. In the 1950s, Branson, Missouri was a sleepy resort town. The area had attracted vacationers for decades for the fishing on Lake Taneycomo and to see the Shepherd of the Hills country popularized by Harold Bell Wright's book published in 1907.

In 1959, Jack Herschend asked Bob if The Baldknobbers would perform at a news conference announcing the opening of Silver Dollar City. The new attraction including Marvel Cave and a recreated 19th century Ozarks village was planned to draw visitors who wanted to enjoy the splendid scenery and experience the culture of the Ozarks. Newly completed nearby Table Rock Lake was bound to add to the coming tourism explosion.

The Baldknobbers with added member Chick Allen, renowned local herbalist, museum operator and jawbone playing musician, were asked to play at Silver Dollar City's opening day in May, 1960. Herschend asked Bob if they had a banjo player which he thought would add to their Ozarkian authenticity. The Baldknobbers didn't have a banjo, so Bob purchased one from a pawn shop in Springfield for $75 and learned to play a few chords over two weeks. Their performances at Silver Dollar City were well received and they continued playing there regularly on weekends.

With their success growing, The Baldknobbers played frequently around Branson, including providing square dance music for the Shepherd of the Hills outdoor play. They made appearances at local craft shows like Plumb Nellie Days.

Bob could see there was a strong demand for authentic Ozark music. He arranged to use the Community Building in Branson, putting on shows six nights a week during the tourist season. Attracting large crowds, The Baldknobbers moved to the old skating rink building on the Taneycomo lakefront. During this period, The Baldknobbers refined their musicianship and their performance. They added Delbert Howard on fiddle. Bob was a natural emcee, standing tall, addressing the crowds of eager tourists with his deep, resonant voice.

"We always tried to stay true to what we believed," Bob says. His group played a variety of music including the old ballads, fiddle tunes and western songs. "We tried to keep the music upbeat, because that's what people liked." True to his Christian beliefs, Bob always included three or four gospel tunes at the end of each show. They kept the basic instruments- guitar, fiddle, Dobro and washboard.

The Baldknobbers began to introduce comedy into their performances. George Agernight would come out from offstage, dressed in stereotypical Ozarks overalls and smile a big, toothless grin. Acting as the straight man, Bob would banter with stuttering George and the crowds loved it. Later, the group added "Droopy Drawers" played by Jim Mabe. Droopy played the washboard and provided intermittent comedy routines. Bob says it took Droopy five years to "learn how to be funny." Under Bob Mabe's direction, The Baldknobbers succeeded in entertaining both locals and visitors in the booming vacation town Branson.

In 1968, The Baldknobbers built a new theater on Highway 76 west of Branson, helping start the growing development that would become "Country Music Boulevard". Bob Mabe's music continued to be true to his roots and his love of both traditional mountain music and more recent country and western tunes.

In 1976, Bob sold his interest in The Baldknobbers to his three brothers. While Bill, Jim and Lyle continued performing as The Baldknobbers, Bob built a new theater and started Bob-O-Links (Bob's nickname) Country Hoedown on West 76.

Bob Mabe continued in the music performance business for several more years. He was instrumental in establishing Branson as a music center over a span of fifty years. When asked what made Ozarks music unique, Bob says, "It's how you do it. You got to be true to what you believe. People will appreciate that. I love to entertain. I've had one of the best lives a person could have. Music has been good to me and I guess I've been good to music." [147]

*The Baldknobbers*

Silver Dollar City opened its doors to the public in 1960. Built on the grounds surrounding Marvel Cave, the Herschends developed a theme park re-creating a "typical" 1880s Ozarks village. The attraction presented several good examples of Ozarks handicrafts and demonstrations of traditional mountain skills. Authentic regional music was performed up and down the steep, wooded walkways of the park. Silver Dollar City also offered amusement park rides with an Ozarks twist, some with silly, stereotyped themes and characters.

The City generally portrayed a positive image and should be congratulated for its presentations of Ozarks handicrafts and music. Over time, the park has become more commercialized and its authenticity has suffered. Silver Dollar City is extremely popular. It has created jobs for hundreds of local people and still offers a selection of Ozarks handicrafts. But the park is a tourist attraction and the carnival-like thrill rides and increasingly non-Ozarks merchandise has rendered Silver Dollar City more a vacation destination and less an advocate for true Ozarks culture.

Back down the road from Silver Dollar City on Highway 76, the Shepherd of the Hills Homestead began productions of

Wright's famous story the same year Silver Dollar City opened, 1960. Developed on the location where Wright was inspired to write *The Shepherd of the Hills*, the Homestead has performed reenactments of the novel for over sixty years. The play remains true to the original work, offering a mostly pleasant, romantic view of the people and culture of the Ozarks.

Down in Arkansas, Dogpatch USA opened its gates in 1968. Situated in beautiful Marble Falls Hollow off picturesque Highway 7, the theme park was entirely based on Al Capp's derogatory stereotypes of his cartoon strip. Although the park was a fun place and probably intended no offense, it did little to recognize or promote a more accurate view of mountain people or their culture. It was just another tourist destination in a region blessed with outstanding scenery.

Dogpatch always struggled to make a profit and after years of inadequate attendance and risky business decisions, it closed for good in 1993. Recently, the Dogpatch property has been purchased by Johnny Morris owner of Bass Pro Shops. It is hoped that Morris will be able to preserve the natural beauty of the Marble Falls area and that any development of the property promotes positive Ozarks culture.

On the very western edge of the Ozarks, Grand Lake o' the Cherokees was formed on the Neosho River in 1940. Near their home on Grand Lake, Harvey and Bernice Jones built a rustic chapel which by 1968 developed into Har-Ber Village. The Village has done a good job recreating a pioneer village and presenting authentic collections of primitive Ozarkiana and Native American artifacts and sponsoring educational programs that help preserve Ozarks skills, arts and crafts. Har-ber Village has avoided amusement park attractions and stayed true to a realistic presentation of Ozarks culture.

Overall, the Ozarks theme parks should probably be given a B- grade for their portrayal of Ozarks culture. They have opened a window for millions of vacationers to experience the Ozarks Highlands and maybe sparked some interest in Ozarks history and culture. The Ozark Folk Center in Mountain View and Har-Ber Village in Grove, Oklahoma are both good examples of attractions that present an accurate view of mountain culture.

But some of the parks have perpetuated hillbilly stereotypes and over-commercialized mountain music and handicrafts. They are businesses however, so perhaps their faults from a cultural standpoint can be given some latitude.

Commercial mountain music venues fall into a similar interpretation. Starting with the "hillbilly" music presented by Okeh Records back in the twenties, the recognition, performance and interpretation of "true" mountain music has run the gamut from ridiculous to sublime.

The music of the hills would be molded and modified. Musicologists like John and Alan Lomax, Vance Randolph, Mary Celestia Parler and Max Hunter collected recordings and transcribed lyrics from Ozarks musicians covering much of the twentieth century. Are these performances true examples of hillbilly music? Probably about as true as can be found. Certainly most of these hill folk had already been influenced by outside factors: traveling troubadours, radio, movies and later television.

The musicians recorded in their homes and sitting on their front porches probably represented true hillbilly music about as accurately as was possible. The early music and folk festivals that started in the 1930s captured the status of hill musicology as it wound its way into a wider national audience. Nationally broadcast programs like the *Grand Ole Opry* and the *Ozark Jubilee* presented some versions of traditional mountain folk music, but these performances were so intertwined with the complex assemblage of country and western and folk that they became lost in the ratatouille of mixed genres.

Adding to the confusion, presentations of mountain music beyond the front porch were still often combined with comedy. There were exceptions. Some musicians like May Kennedy McCord respected the old songs and performed them without the interference of comedic sketches, as did many of those performing at festivals. The resurgence of interest in traditional folk music that began in the 1950s also provided a platform for performance, study and preservation of traditional mountain music. The Rackensack Society made a concerted effort to identify and conserve the art form.

Jimmy Driftwood explained, "In 1963 some people here in Stone County, Arkansas, got together to try to save a part of our American musical heritage. We wanted to encourage the preservation of the folk music that had survived so long in our hills, and our dances and legends, not only for ourselves and our children, but also for our city cousins as well. Much of our folk heritage had been forgotten, drowned out by the jukebox and television. But there were a few people who remembered." [148]

But in the mass media and often even in local commercial ventures, hillbilly music seemed to require the addition of a hill-billy, that is a hillbilly clown. The comic sketches on the *Grand Ole Opry*, a la Elviry and Minnie Pearl, and the *Ozark Jubilee*'s Floyd "Goo Goo" Rutledge were relatively tame compared to some of the rustic comedians who showed up on television in the 1960s and became an important part of the music shows developing in Branson, Missouri.

TV programs like *The Andy Griffith Show*, *Mayberry RFD*, *Petticoat Junction*, *Green Acres* and of course *The Beverly Hillbillies* were extremely popular during the decade of the sixties. Although music generally played a minor role in these shows, they were all rooted in comedy and their portrayals of rural folk were a mixture of teasing, disdain and insult with a dash of country wisdom thrown in.

It is difficult to determine what cultural impact the hillbilly portraitures on these popular programs had. Viewers obviously loved these characters just as they had the vaudeville and min-strel show funnymen. It is very likely that rural viewers ate up these performances as much as urban dwellers. Did the country audience merely enjoy laughing at themselves with the knowl-edge that these comics represented contrived characters? Did the city folk realize that these were really just fabricated depictions? Whatever people were thinking, it is clear that while the come-dy was funny, it was only infrequently offset by more positive characters and behaviors.

*Hee Haw* took the hillbilly stereotype to new levels for both its variety of characters and its longevity of popularity. The pro-gram broadcast new programming from 1969 through 1993 and still can be viewed in syndicated reruns. *Hee Haw* was chock full of nearly every hillbilly stereotype imaginable, from wily tricksters to scantily clad farm girls. Hosted by Buck Owens and Roy Clark for most of its production life, music was always a very important part of the show. And the music was generally well done.

*Hee Haw* was wildly tongue-in-cheek. One could assume that both the players and the audience were laughing with the characters and not at the characters. Though the tropes were extensive and frequent, one could also assume that the viewership got the joke and the "wink wink" from the cast. Or did the program just put another log on the fire of hillbilly bashing?

*The Beverly Hillbillies* played a similar role in television's characterization of comic, but loved rural folk. Spanning most of the 60s, the Clampetts entered the homes of America throughout that tumultuous decade. Perhaps because of his connection to the Ozarks and specifically Branson, producer Paul Henning combined both positive and negative traits in *The Hillbillies'* characters. A bit nicer than Al Capp's Yocum family, the Clampetts included calm, thoughtful patriarch Jed, overbearing, feisty Granny, tall, strong and dumb son Jethro, and voluptuous, kind daughter Elly May.

Although always portrayed in a comic situation, the Clampetts usually outlasted and outwitted their big city neighbors and financial hangers-on. Particularly with Jed, and similar to other television characters like Sheriff Taylor on *The Andy Griffith Show*, the seemingly ignorant hillbilly persona often reveals a great measure of common sense and shrewd wisdom. And again somewhat like Dogpatch's scenarios, the so-called city slickers are revealed to be mercenary and conniving.

Although it is never entirely clear from where the Clampetts originated, a strong connection to the Ozarks was established when five episodes of the program were filmed at Silver Dollar City and aired in 1969. This was a huge boon for Silver Dollar City and the Branson area at large. Henning deserves some credit for at least imbuing the comic *Hillbillies* characters with some endearing, positive traits.

Since its incorporation in 1912, Branson, Missouri has been a tourist mecca. With the completion of the White River Line

Railroad through Branson in 1904 and the creation of Lake Taneycomo in 1913, the town once called Lucia was in an ideal position to attract and entertain vacationers.

Branson was already a stop on White River float trips. The creation of Taneycomo created a whole new opportunity for camps, excursions and outdoor recreation. Mostly attracting upper class enthusiasts from mid-western cities, Branson and its smaller neighbors, Hollister and Rockaway Beach, were well situated to receive, accommodate and provide outdoor adventure for those seeking the bucolic bliss of the Ozark Mountains.

*Lake Taneycomo promotional map*

One of the most successful promoters of Branson was Jim Owen. He started a float fishing business in Branson in 1935 and grew it to be perhaps the most successful regional fishing outfitter; certainly the best promoted and well-known. Owen was a master marketer and he employed his business and advertising background very effectively. He arranged float trips all over the region's rivers, but his most popular trip was the multiple-day float from Galena to Branson.

Jim Owen hired local, colorful guides like Tom Yocum and Little Hoss Jennings to take customers down the free-flowing streams, put them on fish, and regale them with tales of the Ozark hills. Owen made sure national magazines and sports writers covered his business. The Jim Owen Boat Line provided a huge draw to the White River Hills country and introduced thousands of visitors to the joys of Ozarks life until the big lakes covered up the unbridled streams.

Jim Owen understood the impression some of his customers may have harbored about the Ozarks folk. In his typical promoter fashion, he took advantage of the hillbilly image. He opened the Owen Hillbilly Theater on Commercial Street in 1936. Originally used as a movie theater, the site also provided live entertainment for Owen's float trip clients and still exists today as a performance venue.

*Jim Owen's Hillbilly Humor* was published in 1970. If judged by its cover, the book would be just another exercise in tropes. But the content is fairly even-handed with a mix of nostalgia, generic rural humor, and some fun poking at himself and his adopted home town, Branson. Owen shows some understanding when he writes in his book:

"What is a hillbilly? He's been described in various ways—and the dictionary says the term sometimes is used contemptuously—but most of the folks I know around here are proud to be called hillbillies.

Henry F. Rosenthal, an Associated Press staff writer, once wrote an article on the hillbilly based on the fact that one man divorced his wife because—in addition to being bossy and domineering—she called his relatives hillbillies.

According to Rosenthal, a hill resident once told him, 'Hell, boy, any man that rares up at being called a hillbilly just plain ain't one. I'm downright pleased at it.'

To find out what a hillbilly is Rosenthal said, 'You can talk to the real thing by driving through backwood villages on Tight Shoe Day—that's Saturday—when the mountain people put on their good shoes to come to town.'

Rosenthal adds that if it's a question of whether to go coon hunting or tending to business, the hillbilly will go coon hunting.

I agree with him. I've been in these hills since 1933 and I'm just beginning to be accepted as a real hillbilly.

I consider it a compliment because this is the purest Anglo-Saxon blood in the world. The modern hillbilly's kinfolk came to the hills directly from England and retained the old ways. For instance, 'we'uns and you'uns,' still used in the Ozarks, is Elizabethan English.

Rosenthal also said that a hillbilly doesn't get excited about things that worry city people, is shrewd in his dealings and wary of strangers. And he likes to take life easy." [149]

It seems unnecessary that Jim Owen felt he needed to rely on an outlander newspaperman to make his point. Owen had immersed himself in the culture for thirty-five years. He certainly could have made his argument based on his own experiences.

Jim Owen did much to promote the Ozarks and what the region has to offer. He was a booster and certainly much of his motive was mercenary. But his genial manner and generally positive portrayal of Ozarks life did introduce many Americans to the affirmative aspects of mountain culture.

**Jim Owen- float promoter and humorist**

While the building of Bull Shoals, Table Rock and Beaver Lakes may have doomed the float fishing business on the Missouri White River, they opened up a whole new opportunity for promotion and economic improvement for the region. Branson quickly took advantage of this. While Taneycomo became a much colder lake and primarily a trout lake, the big reservoirs provided a multitude of new fishing, boating and camping scenarios.

With the growth of the middle class and improved transportation and communication following World War II, vacationing in the Ozarks was now available to a much larger segment of Americans, not just the wealthy. People came from all over the country to enjoy the lakes and mingle to some degree with the mountain folk. Alongside the outdoor water and woods activities, theme parks and music shows quickly joined the burgeoning vacation playground. Parks like Silver Dollar City, Shepherd of the Hills, Dogpatch and the Arkansaw Traveller Folk Theater in Hardy, Arkansas all became part of the Ozarks vacation experience, offering arts, music and traditional handicrafts at various levels of authenticity.

Keith Thurman can trace his family's roots back multiple generations through Keithley, Moore, Melton and Thurman genealogy. James Willis Archibald Keithley established a settlement on Bear Creek in Taney County, Missouri in 1829 when Osage Indians still roamed the region. Zachariah Moore settled in the same area in 1837 and eventually ran Moore's ferry on the White River. Keith's great-great-great-great grandfather Nathaniel Thurman came to Taney County in the 1830s and possibly even earlier.

Keith's roots run deep in the White River Hills region of the Ozarks. Born in the back bedroom of his grandmother's home near Walnut Shade in 1948, Keith grew up in Rockaway Beach. The resort town on Lake Taneycomo was an exciting place, a small town right on the water that attracted thousands of tourists during the summer months. The Thurmans had operated a riding stable business since the 1930s and Keith took an active role in the enterprise.

Keith says, "When I was about five years old, I'd get on my big ol' black horse and ride from one end of Rockaway to the other, collecting tourists for our trail and stable rides. There were always plenty of takers."

Thurman started a band and played at the dance hall along Beach Boulevard in Rockaway. He met a pretty young girl who was playing the role of Sammy Lane at the Shepherd of the Hills

Theater out on 76 Highway west of Branson. Keith attended performances of the popular live stage show and in 1967, joined the cast as part of the string band in the play's square dance scene. He would go on to play multiple roles in the production and in 1981, took over as director. Thurman has continued to be a part of the theater's productions up to the present.

Thurman says of the play, "Harold Bell Wright wrote a story that has captured people's imaginations for over a hundred years. The Shepherd story is really what put Branson on the map. Early on, some local folks didn't like what he wrote about, but they soon realized just how popular his portrayals were. He really did a pretty fair job of showing what life was like 'round here back then."

Keith Thurman's perspective on the image of the Ozark mountain folk has formed from his family's long lineage in the region and his interactions with locals and tourists through his family's Rockaway business and his long association with the Shepherd of the Hills outdoor drama. He says he didn't hear the term "hillbilly" much growing up until television shows like The Beverly Hillbillies came along. Once at the dinner table, he made a comment about "dumb ol' hillbillies". Usually a quiet man, Keith's father didn't care for the comment at all. His Dad said, "You need to shut up until you know what the hell you're talkin' about. Hillbillies ain't dumb, they're probably the smartest people in the world because you can't come here and be dumb and make it."[150]

Although folk or traditional or hillbilly music had long been part of the culture and attraction of the Ozarks region, the music shows that took off in Branson would establish a whole new interpretation and presentation of mountain music. By the time The Baldknobbers opened their first music show in the Community Building in downtown Branson in 1960, so-called hillbilly music had been sculpted into a melange of genres. Cast into the mix were country, western, bluegrass, gospel, pop, blues, and even rock.

The Baldknobbers helped create a Branson style that included Christian, patriotic and comic themes. It may not have been particularly traditional, but it certainly became popular with the vacation crowd. Quickly to follow were shows like the Presleys and the Plummers. As Branson grew, snaking west out Country Music Boulevard, music shows multiplied and all types of entertainment were added to attract the mass crowds of the "Branson Boom".

Many of the homegrown and imported Branson music shows included a good measure of hillbilly humor. Interspersed into these music performances were comic figures like the Baldknobbers' "Droopy Drawers", the Presleys' "Herkimer", and the Plummer's "Nearly Famous". These funnymen relied primarily on low humor and fell back on old cliches. They occasionally incorporated elements of country wisdom, but the primary impression conveyed was that of a simpleton.

The Branson music phenomenon helped attract millions of people to the Ozarks. Many of these people returned regularly and some decided to make the Ozarks their permanent or retirement home. This in-migration has been an important element in economic development of the region. It may have sparked some interest in traditional Ozarks culture, but newcomers have not always been presented a fair or balanced image. Ultimately, it is up to the participant to decide if the amusement parks, music shows and crafts shops offer an accurate presentation of hillbilly culture.

Keith Thurman who can trace his family's roots back two hundred years in the Ozarks and was associated with the Shepherd of the Hills Outdoor Theater for fifty years puts it well:

"So, that's the real hillbilly that's here, and the perceived hillbilly that's put out to the country were absolutely two totally different things. If you were from here, and somebody called you a hillbilly that lived here, that's fine, but some dumb shit that rolled in here and started talkin' about hillbillies and how dumb they are and this and that, then that wasn't accepted worth a damn, except if you owned a theatre in town. So yeah, we've always been perceived as dumb and lazy, and that's the last thing on earth that a man could be that actually was born and raised in this area. You had to be on top of that or you wouldn't make it." [151]

Josh Heston, founder of stateoftheozarks.net, bemoans the erosion of "true" Ozarks culture he sees taking place in his adopted hometown, Branson. "Branson adopted the hillbilly image and has been very successful in using it as a tourism marketing tool. But that's beginning to fade away. As we become more and more a homogenized society, many of the valuable traits and lore of the Ozarks mountain folk are fading away. In some ways, I think we may have lost our way."[152]

Compared to the first half of the twentieth century, there are definitely fewer movies in the fifty years following World War II that deal with rural characters. The films that do are generally better produced and give their characters more depth and humanity. Although television seemed to love the silly hillbilly as it did in the sixties, the comic rustic began to fade away on the big screen. Rather, many films that approached country life portrayed the mountain person as good or bad.

There are certainly films that dealt with complicated characters like those in Robert Mitchum's *Thunder Road* in 1958 (a tale of moonshiners) and complicated situations like those in 1960's *Wild River* (about conflict between mountain landowners and the TVA).

But there are two films that sit at the extremes.

Perhaps one of the most beloved and popular novels/films that deals directly with Ozarks mountain folk is *Where the Red Fern Grows*. Written by Wilson Rawls and published in 1961, this book has become required reading in many middle schools and remains very popular.

*The Red Fern* is a semi-autobiographical story about a young boy living in the Ozarks (the Oklahoma portion). The romantic and often sad tale describes a young boy's love of the land and coon hunting. The lad, Billy, works hard to purchase two coonhounds and then trains them to be topnotch hunters. The companionship and adventures of Billy and his dogs wind through the thrills and hardships of Ozarks life and the coon hunting experience.

Although perhaps a bit sentimental, Rawl's story is inspiring and believable. He presents his rural characters in a realistic light and the triumphs and struggles of Billy, his family and their country neighbors ring true and authentic. *Where the Red Fern Grows* is a good example of a story written by an Ozarker that presents an honest, positive portrayal of Ozarks living. The book has been produced as a film several times.

In contrast is *Deliverance*. What *Jaws* did to the shark, *Deliverance* did to the hillbilly. Written by James Dickey in 1970 and released as a film in 1972, *Deliverance* was both a box office and critical success. But it did untold damage to the hillbilly image.

Dickey was an accomplished writer, poet and college professor. He was the eighteenth United States Poet Laureate. His novel *Deliverance* is a tale of modern man facing primitive challenges. The movie directed by John Boorman stylizes the story which takes place on a wild, free flowing river in northern Georgia. The main roles, four city fellows, interact with both the wilderness landscape and the denizens of the mountain country.

The rural folk portrayed in the movie are given almost exclusively negative traits. In fact, they are portrayed as smartass antagonists, in-bred and mentally deficients, savage killers and rapists. Dickey himself has a cameo appearance in the film as the surly local sheriff. The only positive depictions come at the very end of the movie when some local folk assist the assailed protagonists.

*Deliverance* is an exciting horror film, but it continues to convey offensive, horrendous attributes to the hillbilly image. The music, lines and scenes from the movie are to this day regurgitated as "warnings" against the threats and dangers of the mountain folk and their environment.

Somewhere between *Red Fern* and *Deliverance* is the work of novelist Donald Harington. Although not a native to the Ozark Highlands (he was born and raised in Little Rock) he did spend time as a youth at his grandparents' home in Drakes Creek, deep in the Boston Mountains.

Haringtom wrote several novels from 1970 to 2009 that either take place in or have a connection to the fictional Ozarks backwater town of Stay More. Harington's story lines and characters are complex and approach the hillbilly personae and culture in an open minded, nonjudgmental fashion. He freely delves into the passions, motives and foibles of the provocative folk that reside in and move through Stay More. Sometimes Harington's characters and plotlines can be shocking, sexual and bizarre. But they are always original and interesting. Perhaps by their exceptionalism, the people of Stay More are made all that much more human and akin to every other human being.

In the introduction to *The Nearly Complete Works of Donald Harrington* Peter Straub reveals perhaps some of the source for Harington's originality: [153]

"Harington beautifully described this bittersweet, ambivalent process in a 1994 interview published in the *Appalachian Journal*. 'I am too educated to be a hillbilly…I forfeit my hillbilliness in order to write novels about hillbillies. It is some consolation that certain characteristics of hillbillies—fierce independence, shyness coupled with loquacity, a wry if not sardonic humor—remain in my bloodstream, remain in my genes, and permit me never to forget what it is like being a hillbilly, at the same time that they deprive me of complete objectivity about hillbillies. I can't laugh about hillbillies because I am still laughing with them.'"

Donald Harington has received critical acclaim for his body of work, but is probably lesser known than other Ozarks writers. His stories of Stay More certainly deserve a look for their originality and unusual window into the mind and behavior of the Ozarks highlander.

Steve Seaton says he grew up living a self-described "hillbilly life". "We were poor, but we had a lot of fun. I was raised a hillbilly and I'm proud of it."

The Seaton family has experienced the vicissitudes of Ozarks living for decades. Steve's grandfather Howard Mort Seaton was a Missouri Pacific railroad engineer on the White River Line between Crane, Missouri and Cotter, Arkansas. His grandmother's family the Snyders owned a boarding house in Cotter, which was lost during the Depression. Settling in Crane, Howard and Lula Seaton began raising their family.

Steve's father Bruce grew up in Crane, but after serving in the Merchant Marine during World War II, he moved often as a young man. Bruce met his bride Dorthy in Carthage where Steve was born. Eventually, Bruce moved his family back to Stone County, Missouri in 1963. He purchased property and built a modest home that came to be known as the "old home place" where the eight Seaton children grew up. Bruce Seaton was a self-made man trying his hand at multiple jobs: truck farming, a dairy operation, timber logging and even cattle breeding. Eventually, Bruce commuted to school in Columbia and learned the printing business.

Bruce worked for local newspapers and then landed a job working in the print shop at Silver Dollar City. Seaton had a creative mind. His gregarious personality led him to realize the potential of tourism in the Ozarks. In the mid-60s, Bruce Seaton combined his skills in photography, printing and salesmanship into a marketable business. He set up vignettes in front of their tar-papered home or nearby ramshackle structures. The entire family dressed and posed in stereotypical "hillbilly" depictions. "We really got into these set-ups," Steve says. "We knew they were silly stereotypes, but we had a lot of fun with it. And my Dad knew these photos had commercial value."

The Seaton photos were developed into postcards and calendars and the merchandise took off. The Seaton's family photos sold well around the Ozarks and were even distributed internationally. The scenes depicted played on the expected characteristics of the hillbilly image. The corncob pipe smoking women did all the work with help from the shabbily dressed girls. The men and boys in overalls slouched and held jugs of moonshine.

Steve says, "Some people took offense to the images we created. They were exaggerated and didn't really represent our way of life. We all worked hard. We were poor and everybody chipped in to make ends meet."

The Seatons also played roles in the outdoor play at Shepherd of the Hills Homestead. Bruce Seaton performed as Preachin' Bill and the Sheriff in the production from 1961 to 1976. In the 1960s, Steve was cast as Deputy Bob while his brother Mark played the role of Little Pete. Dorthy taught and participated in the square dance scenes and helped with the play's production for forty-nine years.

Bruce Seaton passed away in 1976 at the age of forty-nine. His family continued on the Seaton tradition of hard work and promoting Ozarks lore. They eventually sold the rights to their images and the hillbilly calendar is still produced.

The Seatons did not get wealthy from the hillbilly scenes they created. In some ways they lived their lives as "intentional hillbillies", working multiple jobs to support themselves, living a rustic lifestyle, and depicting roles that the tourists expected to see. The characters they portrayed in print belie their true existence. The hillbilly calendars played on the stereotypes that many outlanders had come to apply to the mountain folk. Like Jim Owen, the Baldknobbers music show and many other local entrepreneurs, the Seatons employed the hillbilly image for its commercial value. But this imagined lifestyle is most often quite removed from the reality of Ozarks life.

*Seaton "Hillbilly Calendar" image*

Bruce and Dorthy Seaton's children have led successful, positive lives. Steve Seaton lives in Hurley with his wife Beni where he enjoys gardening and creating curiosities out of everyday items. He has served as Mayor of Hurley and works with the Stone County Historical Society and Library Board. [154]

The Ozarks as a vacation land created two dissimilar views of its culture. The visitors who had travelled here for decades to enjoy the scenery and outdoor sports were enthralled by the region's beauty and friendly, welcoming people. But they also seemed to buy into the stereotyped portrayals and the natives' otherness. The dichotomy persisted that the hillbilly on one hand was a loveable, proud mountaineer and on the other, a poor rube or worse, a dangerous savage. These opposing images were perpetuated by outlander writers, national media, and even the mountain folk themselves at times.

The Ozarks region had long attracted temporary visitors who came for the hunting and fishing camps, the mineral springs of "healing water", and the long-term camping resorts. Although these visitors probably thought they were "roughing it", they were usually experiencing the hill country in a created setting. Most of the resorts attempted to provide as much comfort and modern conveniences as possible. Most interaction with locals was limited to guide and domestic services. It is probable that the vacationers returned home with pleasant memories of the Ozarks. But these experiences still had to compete with the stereotypes the national media loved to throw around.

Perhaps the vacationer can be given some leeway in accepting these constructs — after all, their time in the hills was limited and they tended to stay within the confines of the lakes, campgrounds and amusement venues. But some of these vacationers eventually relocated to the Ozarks. Some came to live in a more rural, less stressful environs and some came to retire here. The influx of people into the Ozarks region changed both the newcomers and the Ozarkers.

Vance Randolph gives a rather depressing opinion on the impact of modernization and tourism on the Ozarks as early as 1931: [155]

"It is no wonder that the best minds among the hill people resent the invasion of outside interests. Great corporations taking their timber and their water-power, and their neglected little farms are fast falling into alien and more efficient hands. Their old neighbors are moving out, and new and unwelcome ones are coming in. Many of the most prosperous farmers and the most enterprising merchants in the Ozarks nowadays are not natives at all. The rapidly growing tourist and resort business is practically controlled by 'furriners'. The best of the mountain boys and girls leave this under-privileged region and go to the cities; only the culls are left in the hill country, and these are regularly prone to imitate the follies and vices of the sky-larking tourists."

The development of the Ozarks as a relocation and retirement destination began in the early twentieth century with the promise by the boosters of cheap land, clean air and water, and a bucolic lifestyle. Boosters like Otto Rayburn made it their goal to inform readers about the region's positive attributes and encouraged them to relocate to a less stressful homeland. Some of Rayburn's enthusiasm can be attributed to his desire to sell publications and real estate. But there is no doubt that he believed what he promoted and truly felt that the Ozarks had much to offer.

Rayburn wrote in flowing terms his description of an Ozarkian Arcadia: [156]

"Wayfaring in the Ozarks! What delightful adventure, what rollicking humor, what flavor of hospitality! Rustic innocence, untroubled quiet, pastoral simplicity! Here in Arcadia in the closing years of the fourth decade of the twentieth century."

Commercial development played a significant role in attempts to attract people to the Ozarks. Spurred on by the Country Life Movement and potential tourist dollars, business groups began to organize advertising campaigns early in the twentieth century. In 1913, William Harvey helped create the Ozark Trails Association with the goal of improving Ozarks roads, specifically those roads leading to his Monte Ne project in northwest Arkansas. The OTA sought funding from the states of Oklahoma, Kansas, Missouri and Arkansas and published regional maps and tourism brochures. The OTA achieved limited success with road improvements, at least partially due to Harvey's obstinacy. By the 1920s, they had ceased operations.

In 1919, Joplin commercial interests formed the Ozark Playgrounds Association. Their intent was to attract tourists, businesses and economic development to thirteen counties in southwest Missouri and northwest Arkansas. The group's slogan was "The Land of a Million Smiles", playing on a romanticized sketch of the Ozarks Highlands. The OPA produced ads, postcards and travel guides and marketed them throughout the Midwest. The Playgrounds' efforts were reasonably successful and they continued functioning until the 1970s.

*The Land of a Million Smiles*

The Ozarks boosters were moderately successful in attracting tourist dollars during the early 1900s. Roads remained almost impassable until the 1920s. The railroads did provide adequate transportation to some areas and the resort communities near railway stations were able to draw wealthier clients for fishing, hunting and long term cabin rentals. There was considerable improvement to roads and bridges during the Roaring Twenties. The publication of *The Shepherd of the Hills* acted as an inadvertent marketing advertisement for many vacationers.

The Ozarks continued pulling in well-to-do customers through the 1920s, but the Depression era and World War II dampened the influx of Ozark-seeking adventurers. A few hardy souls abided by Otto Rayburn's guidance and sought out permanent dwelling in the high hills and deep valleys. But these romantic escapades were often short-lived.

Charlie May Simon was one of those who sought out a bucolic lifestyle deep in the Arkansas highlands. In 1931, Simon and her husband homesteaded sixty acres near where her grandfather had established a farm some sixty-six years earlier. Charlie May was no stranger to a hard scrabble life as she was born on a tenant farm. She married a wealthy man and enjoyed a sophisticated life as a young woman, but the rural life drew her.

Published in 1945, *Straw In The Sun* is Simon's story of the four years they lived in the backwoods home they built at Rocky Comfort. How much of her novel is fictionalized is moot (Simon's husband Howard is never mentioned in her book). Simon's story is so well-told in beautiful, flowing words that its honesty and accuracy are undeniable.

*Straw In The Sun* relates the difficulty and the joy of living a simple, rugged life. Simon recounts all the traits and characteristics that reflect the environment, the people and the ethos of mountain living. Her story is sad, uplifting and forthright.

Simon's admiration for her mountain neighbors is obvious when she writes:[157]

"Those were the poor whites, the Wheelers, the Nixons, the Wells and the Widow Johnson. People who live in unpainted shacks and go barefoot in the summer, who wear patched clothes and smell of sweat and tobacco and cotton cloth. In some states they are called "Peckerwoods' or "Crackers'. Cartoons are drawn about them and plays are written about them to make people laugh. But I lived through the rest of that winter, knowing a kindness and a generosity I had never known before, when, in their poverty, they shared the little they had with me and among themselves."

Charlie May Simon is best known for her several notable children's books. She is honored through the annual Charlie May Simon Children's Book Award. But for a clear-eyed portrayal of mountain folk and their character, *Straw In The Sun* is a worthy account.

The period between the wars actually saw extensive out-migration from the Ozarks. Many hillfolk either left temporarily to work in the industrial cities or migrant farm jobs. Some never returned. Others lost their homesteads to foreclosure and were forced to leave permanently. Even following World War II, the Ozarks continued to lose residents. "During the 1950s alone, the region [the Ozarks] experienced a net loss of 431,000 people, most of them young adults who sought economic opportunities elsewhere." [158] Despite the out-migration, attempts continued to attract new people to the mountain region, both as temporary visitors and as permanent residents.

In 1900, William "Coin" Harvey purchased 320 acres of Ozarks valley land at the site of an old grist mill southeast of Rogers and just off the White River. Harvey was a well-known financier, politician and writer. He widely promoted his support of silver coinage and was a proponent of William Jennings Bryan in the 1896 presidential election. Harvey was himself a presidential candidate for President in 1932 as the leader of the Liberty Party.

Harvey's political ambitions were unsuccessful and he retreated to his Arkansas refuge. He devised grand plans to develop the property into a resort and sanctuary from the ills of modern society. Naming his project Monte Ne, Harvey did complete several large amenities including three huge log hotels, a railroad spur to the property, the first indoor swimming pool in Arkansas, and a dance pavilion. The resort did attract a clientele of wealthier customers who could afford the travel and accommodations expense. But Harvey's dreams were larger than reality.

Despite his major financial investment and marketing efforts, outlays surpassed revenues and by 1917, Monte Ne was essentially bankrupt. With personal, financial and political losses, "Coin's" thinking became more eccentric. He devised a plan to build an amphitheater and pyramid at Monte Ne. The pyramid (or more accurately an obelisk) was to contain a time capsule capturing the symbols of twentieth century achievement. Harvey espoused the belief that civilization had reached its pinnacle, would soon decline and that his pyramid would be a "permanent" receptacle for mankind's achievement.

Due to inadequate planning and investment, the pyramid was never completed. Monte Ne's facilities continued to function under different owners and for various uses. William Harvey died in 1936 and was entombed in a concrete mausoleum at Monte Ne. When Beaver Lake was completed in 1965, the White River's waters crept up and over most of Monte Ne. Harvey's tomb was relocated to higher ground, but everything else was inundated. Now under low lake levels, some portions of the amphitheater and the incomplete pyramid are visible along the lake's shoreline. The remains are a ghostly reminder of Coin Harvey's dream. [159]

*Monte Ne*

One of the first largescale, planned communities in the Ozarks was Bella Vista in Benton County, Arkansas. Originally foreseen as a seasonal recreation area, William and Mary Baker purchased a tract of rough, forested land in 1915, created a lake, and offered lots for sale with envisioned amenities.

The Baker's plans did not immediately succeed and the property was purchased by the Linebarger family in 1916. The Linebargers proceeded to develop Bella Vista, making improvements and adding a lodge, golf course and swimming pool. The resort was successful in attracting wealthy, urban dwellers who sought long-term summer vacations.

The Depression and World War II saw a decline in Bella Vista's fortunes and the property was sold to Elzy Lloyd Keith in 1952. John A. Cooper started investing in Bella Vista lots in 1965. His venture was very successful. By 2006, Cooper had sold 38,000 home sites and 12,600 were developed. Bella Vista became not only a vast retirement community, it was eventually incorporated as a city and exists today as an exurb to the burgeoning northwest Arkansas metropolis. [160]

John Cooper was also the developer of Cherokee Village along the South Fork River near Hardy, Arkansas. Based on Cooper's love of the region's natural attraction, Cherokee Village, founded in 1954, was one of the first and largest planned retirement communities in the country. Today, the resort covers 15,000 acres and has nearly 5,000 full-time residents and 15,000 property owners. [161]

The Narrows is a thin land bridge between the White River and Leatherwood Creek at Beaver, Arkansas that connects to a large, triangular-shaped peninsula now called Holiday Island.

This chunk of land was first settled by Hughey and Susannah Bandy in the 1850s. They called the property The Bottom Place, but it eventually became known as Bandy's Bend. Hughey's daughter Mary Ann married Felix Grundy Burnett in 1868 and the couple named the family farm The Homestead Place. Members of the Burnett family are buried in a small cemetery preserved on the "island".

Richard Shields, a Kansas oilman, purchased the Burnett land in 1938 and developed it into a horse ranch called Palisades Farm. Chicago banker Henry S. Banach bought the ranch in 1954 and promoted it as a "fisherman's paradise" resort. Following the construction of Table Rock Lake, McCullough Corporation developed the peninsula as Holiday Island, now a thriving community and residential area with over 2000 residents. [162]

In addition to the efforts of commercial boosters and the development of large retirement communities, some Ozarks in-migration occurred as a result of a small, recurrent back-to-the-land movement. Originally an offshoot of the Country Life and Arcadian crusades, relocation to a quieter, simpler rural life saw some resurgence following World War II.

Julia McAdoo and her husband, seeking their own Arcadian dream in 1953, bought a tract of land 'in the hills of Northern Arkansas'. In an article for *American Mercury*, she extolled the virtuous people whom she had come to call her neighbors.

"In these secluded hills where telephones are rare, and roads are bare of traffic, where jobs are few and industry unknown, lives a race, a people, quite different from most. Unimpressed by riches, unafraid of poverty, serene, not humble and not proud. These 'hillbillies', these woodsmen, have no set standard of living, no respect for money, nor fame, nor caste. They know no greed, no envy, no subserviency. These unimpressive men in unimpressive garb, though poor they seem, are immensely rich.'" [163]

In the 1960s and 1970s, "back-to-the-landers" came to the Ozarks as part of the counter-culture movement. Often labeled as "hippies", these newcomers came to the hills to find a peaceful, rustic existence and to escape the materialism and prejudice of so-called mainstream society. They also sought an existence that was more in tune with nature and environmentally sound. [164]

These Arcadian immigrants were relatively small in number, but they strove hard to establish rural lives that were in some ways akin to those of the Ozarks pioneers. They embraced the bucolic beauty of the Ozarks highlands while grappling with the rigors of establishing successful farms in the poor Ozarks soil. The back to the landers were sometimes at odds with the mores and lifestyles of the local populace. But they also connected with the traditions and independent thinking of the hill folk.

These counter-culture in-migrants developed relationships with and learned useful skills from their neighbors and over time had some influence on the region's attitudes regarding education, childbirth and child rearing, and environmental issues.

Jared Phillips calls these mid-twentieth century homesteaders "hipbillies" and says, "The hipbillies were another wave of people at once both enamored with, and empowered by, the mythology of the Ozarks; so much so that they found the wherewithal to root themselves deep in the hills and build the world they envisioned. While they did not always succeed, the story is not over—they are still alive and are still powerful cultural, political, and economic forces in the Arkansas highlands." [165]

Along with the "back to the land" movement of the 1960s and 70s, there was a renewed interest in all things rustic and primitive. Although the Ozarks culture and its people had been irreversibly altered by this time, they were still viewed as a source for old time music, skills and crafts. Some merely wanted to see these archaic forms, while others hoped to preserve them. Historical societies, folk festivals, and to some degree tourist destinations promulgated varying degrees of authentic Ozarks arts and crafts.

Ellen Gray Massey, English teacher at Lebanon High School in Missouri sought to preserve some of the Ozarks culture through education. Author of several books, including the Mary Elizabeth Mahnkey biography *A Candle Within Her Soul*, Massey assigned her students the task of creating a magazine exploring some of the dying Ozarks arts and crafts.

The students sought out contacts who still knew and practiced these primitive skills. The resultant *Bittersweet* magazine, published quarterly from 1973 to 1983, covered all manner of mountain crafts from hog butchering to tie hacking to traditional music. *Bittersweet* did a good job of capturing and preserving these skills as well as endowing its creators and readers with a respect for these "old" ways.

The level of interest in these fading arts reveals a new-found appreciation for "hillbilly" culture. Now that they were harder to find, the old ways attracted a new fascination. Capturing what it took to create and maintain a home, provide sustenance, care for the sick and dying and maintain a positive existence were now acknowledged and admired.

The building of the Corps of Engineers lakes created a significant in-migration of new residents to the Ozarks region. Thousands came to vacation and eventually build a summer home. Many moved here permanently. By the 1960s, there were little of the "old" Ozarks ways left. Years of interaction, modernization, and improved economies had so altered the mountain culture that it had become at worse an anachronism and at best, a cherished tradition.

The image of the hillbilly had been assuaged by improvements to rural life, homogenization of lifestyles and interaction between mountain folk and the wider world. There remains some of the comic representations, particularly in country music, and the tendency to apply political beliefs to a broad rural populace. But the widespread assignation of negative "hillbilly" stereotypes to hillfolk has waned some.

There are still those who will make the occasional "Deliverance" joke and those who will consider someone of lesser economic status or perceived lesser sophistication as "others". Two centuries of distorted chronicling, reporting, representations and stereotyping do not fade rapidly. It is only through thorough analysis, study and direct experience that one can begin to have a fuller understanding of the hillbilly's background, lifestyle and cultural existence.

This study of the source, development and portrayals of the hillbilly character has sought to broaden the interpretation and add some understanding to why the stereotypes arose and why they festered for so long. The stories of individuals who were born and raised or spent considerable portions of their lives in the Ozarks Mountain country reveal personalities that are complex and imbued with positive traits.

These folk forged decent, successful lives out of the rock-strewn hills and hollows. Their character and behavior were molded by their environment and the nurture of their family and close neighbors. Buoyed by hereditary and cultural attributes, the mountain folk initially adapted to a fairly isolated existence. Their traditions sustained them.

Over time as the region became more settled and towns and cities grew, mountain culture clung to the old ways, but could not avoid the processes of acculturalization and homogenization through interaction. Particularly at the beginning of the twentieth century, as communications and transportation improved, the hillfolk slowly adopted modernization. Some may have resisted these changes, but change was inevitable.

A way of life based on hunting, gathering and subsistence farming became less tenable. Mountain people had to find ways to adapt to modernization and new economies. Many left the hills either temporarily or permanently. Many were forced from their land through eviction or bankruptcy. Many did stay and accepted new ways of living a mountain life.

These folk did not necessarily eschew their traditions and culture. But it became harder and harder to sustain and pass on their lore and customs. The outside world beckoned the young and the old ways became associated with old folk. Identifying and preserving this folk culture was embraced by some, both inlanders and outlanders. And there has been and still is some success in conserving the Ozarks folkways. If we are serious about conserving these traditions, we must be honest about the true portrait of the mountain identity and reject the stereotyped images so rife in our society.

The hillbilly persona developed out of stilted perceptions portrayed by the chroniclers, outlander writers and journalists, and the mass media of music, films and novels. In some cases, Ozarkers bought into these portrayals, particularly the comic ones, and employed them for commercial benefit. But too often, these negative perceptions were accepted as descriptive of the whole of the Ozarks populace. It became just too easy to assign pejorative attributes to a people misunderstood and label them as "others".

As we have seen, many Ozarkers will accept the hillbilly moniker as a compliment because they know what it means to strive and struggle in a harsh land. But they also realize that the name calling carries a mean-spirited insult — it is all about context.

Perhaps we should relegate the "h" word to history and the study of mountain culture and lore. We cannot forget it, but we cannot accept it.

# Endnotes

1    From personal interviews with Wanda (Villines) Donaldson March 8, 2021 and April 5, 2021

2    Harris, Nathaniel, *Heritage of Scotland A Cultural History of Scotland & Its People*, Octopus Publishing Group Limited, London, 2000. p.76

3    ibid, p.74

4    *The Ozark Region Its History and Its People*, Volume 1, Interstate Historical Society, Springfield, Mo., 1917, p.79

5    From a personal interview with Josh Heston, January 20, 2021

6    https://www.scotclans.com/scottish-clans/the-clan-system/

7    ibid

8    *Arkansas' Ozark Mountain Blacks: An Introduction*, Gordon D. Morgan and Peter Kunkel, *Phylon (1960)* Vol. 34, No. 3 (3rd Qtr., 1973), pp. 283-288, published by: Clark Atlanta University

9    Blevins, Brooks, *Hill Folks A History of Arkansas Ozarkers and Their Image*, The University of North Carolina Press, 2002

10   Randolph, Vance, *The Ozarks An American Survival of Primitive Society*, The University of Arkansas Press, Fayetteville, 2017, edited by Robert Cochran, p.60, originally published in 1931

11   Randolph, Vance, and Wilson, George P., *Down in the Holler: A Gallery of Ozark Folk Speech*, University of Oklahoma Press, 1953, pp. 72-3

12   "Hillbilly", West Virginia Encyclopedia, www.wvencyclopedia.org, 2020

13   Hawthorne, Julian (April 23, 1900*). "*Mountain Votes Spoil Huntington's Revenge*". New York Journal: 2.

14   Montgomery, Michael, *From Ulster to America The Scotch-Irish Heritage of American English*, Ulster Historical Foundation, 2006, p.82

15   *"Hillbilly' is a derogatory term to some, but it's embraced by America's Scotch-Irish descendants"*, The Sun newspaper, Lowell, MA, July 11, 2019

16   Green, James, *The Devil is Here in These Hills*, Atlantic Monthly Press, 2015

17   Wilkinson, Todd J., Scottish Tartans Authority, "Hillbillies and Rednecks", www.tartansauthority.com

18   https://www.yesmagazine.org/economy/2015/05/20/is-west-virginia-s-coal-history-a-goldmine-mine-wars/

19   Wilkinson, Todd J., Scottish Tartans Authority, "Hillbillies and Rednecks", tartansauthority.com, quoting *King John*, William Shakespeare, 1595

20   Randolph, Vance, *Down in the Holler*, ibid

21   Schoolcraft, Henry Rowe, *Journal Of a Tour Into the Interior of Missouri and Arkansas 1818-1819*, Richard Phillips and Company, 1821

22   Bolton, S. Charles, *Territorial Ambition Land and Society in Arkamsas*

*1800-1840*, The University of Arkansas Press, Fayetteville, 1993, pp.34-5
23  Featherstonhaugh, George William, *Excursion Through the Slave States*, Harper, New York, 1844, p.96
24  Gerstaeker, Frederick, *Wild Sports in the Far West*, Crosby, Nichols and Company, Boston, 1859, p.172
25  Hogan, Rev. John J., *On the Mission in Missouri 1857-1868*, Kansas City, John A. Heilmann, 1892
26  Blevins, Brooks, *Arkansas/Arkansaw How Bear Hunters, Hillbillies and Good Ol' Boys Defined a State*, University of Arkansas Press, 2009, p.25
27  Ibid, Chapters 1 and 2
28  Read, Opie P., *Up Terrapin River*, Rand, McNally & Co. 1888, p.5
29  Emory Melton, *Delaware Town and the Swan Trading Post 1822-1831*, court transcript, Litho Printers, Cassville, Mo., p.14
30  Melton, *ibid*, pp. 26-7
31  From a personal interview with Ben Loftin January 31, 2006
32  Koob, Tom, *Buried By Table Rock Lake*, White Oak Lodge Publishing, 2008, pp 68-71
33  Townsend, Godsey and Helen, *Ozarks Mountain Folk These Were The Last*, Land Press, Inc., Branson, Mo, 1977, Introduction, p.15
34  Randolph, Vance, *Ozark Superstitions*, Columbia University Press, New York, 1947, p.3
35  ibid, p.6
36  ibid, p.100
37  ibid, p.178
38  ibid, pp.180-1
39  Rayburn, Otto Ernest, "The Granny-Woman in the Ozarks", *Midwest Folklore*, Vol. 9, No. 3 Autumn 1959, pp.147-8, Indiana University Press, quoting May Kennedy McCord's "Hillbilly Heartbeats" column in the *Springfield Daily News*
40  Horner, Irene, *Roaring River Heritage*, Litho Printers, 1978, pp. 23-4
41  Randolph, Vance, *Ozark Magic and Folklore*, Columbia University Press, 1947, p.5
42  ibid, pp.278-9
43  "Eureka Springs", www.encyclopediaofarkansas.net
44  Asher, Ruth Henson, *White River Valley Historical Quarterly*, Volume 2, Spring 1966, #7
45  Emory Melton identifies Philibert's wife as Peninah and the date of their marriage as 1833. Philibert died in 1884. Melton, Emory, *Delaware Town and the Swan Trading Post 1822-1831*, Litho Printers, Cassville, Mo.
46  Koob, Tom, *Enon to Radium Spring*, White Oak Lodge Publishing, 2008, p. 141-2
47  Ball, Faye (Maloney) and Gaede, Darla (Ball), *Our Easleys*, 1972

48 From a personal interview with Jewel Farwell December 6, 2005

49 Noland, C. F. M., *Cavorting on the Devil's Fork*, edited by Leonard Williams, Memphis State University Press, 1979, pp.194-5, originally published in *The Spirit of the Times*, "Pete Whetstone and the Mail Boy", 1853

50 Thorpe, Thomas Bangs, "The Big Bear of Arkansas", *Spirit of the Times*, 1841

51 ibid

52 Byrn, M. L., *The Life and Adventures of an Arkansaw Doctor*, edited by W.K. McNeil, The University of Arkansas Press, Fayetteville, 1989, an excerpt from Chapter XV

53 Pike, Albert, "Letters from Arkansas", *American Monthly Magazine*, 1835

54 Hogan, Father John, *On the Mission in Missouri, 1857-1868,* J.A. Heilman, Kansas City, Mo., 1892

55 Crawford, Mike, "Father Hogan's 1859 Irish Wilderness Settlement", *The Prospect-News*, Doniphan, Mo., 1993, Exhibit 15

56 Payton, Leland and Crystal, *Mystery of the Irish Wilderness*, Lens and Pen Press, Springfield, MO, 2008

57 Bailey, Anne J. and Sutherland, Daniel E, editors, *Civil War Arkansas Beyond Battles and Leaders*, The University of Arkansas Press, Fayetteville, 2000, Chapter 2

58 Turnbo, Silas C., "Bad Treatment Followed by Revenge", *Fireside Stories of the Early Days in the Ozarks.* Vol. 2, 1907

59 Howard, Rebecca Ann, *Civil War Unionists and Their Legacy in the Arkansas Ozarks*, a dissertation submitted in partial fulfillment of the requirements for the degree of Doctor of Philosophy in History, Texas A&M University Bachelor of Arts in History, Texas A&M University, December 2015, University of Arkansas, p.99

60 Bailey, Anne J. and Sutherland, Daniel E, ibid, Chapter 7, p.137

61 Shea, William L., *Civil War Arkansas Beyond Battles and Leaders*, eds. Anne J. Bailey and Daniel E. Sutherland, "A Semi-savage State: The Image of Arkansas in the Civil War", The University of Arkansas Press, Fayetteville, 2000, Chapter 4, p.88

62 ibid, pp. 88-9

63 Barnes, Kenneth C., *Civil War Arkansas Beyond Battles and Leaders*, eds. Anne J. Bailey and Daniel E. Sutherland, "The Williams Clan: Mountain Farmers and Union Fighters in North Central Arkansas", Chapter 8, The University of Arkansas Press, Fayetteville, 2000

64 ibid, p.175

65 Mahnkey, Douglas, "Troubles in Taney County- 1880s", *White River Valley Historical Quarterly*, Volume 9. Number 5. Fall 1986

66    Kalen, Kristen and Morrow, Lynn,    "Nat Kinney's Sunday School Crowd", *White River Valley Historical Quarterly*, Volume 33, Number 1, Fall 1993

67    Morrow, Lynn, "Where Did All the Money Go? War and the Economics of Vigilantism in Southern Missouri", *White River Valley Historical Quarterly*, Volume 34, Number 2, Fall, 1994

68    Perkins, J. Blake, *Hillbilly Hellraisers Federal Power and Populist Defiance in the Ozarks*, University of Illinois Press, 2017, Chapter 2

69    ibid, Chapter 2

70    ibid, p.61

71    "George Ray Lilly" by Brad Melton, 2018

72    Cunningham, B. and Hauser, C., "The decline of the Missouri Ozark Forest between 1880 and 1920", Journet, A.R.P., H.G. Spratt, Jr., ed., 1992

73    www.ladfoundation.org

74    Auckley, Jim, "The Boat Builder From White River", *Missouri Conservationist* magazine, revised October 21, 2010

75    ibid

76    ibid

77    Rossiter, Phyllis,    *A Living History of the Ozarks*, Pelican Publishing Company, 1992, p.139

78    Koob, Tom, *Buried By Table Rock Lake*, White Oak Lodge Publishing, 2006, from personal interviews with Scotty Chamberlin, January 16, 2006 and February 3, 2007

79    Wright, Harold Bell, *The Shepherd of the Hills*, Grosset & Dunlap, New York, 1907, pp. 25-6

80    The Anti-Horse Thief Association was established in 1854 in Clark County, Mo. by Major David McKee. The organization was founded to combat horse thievery and general lawlessness. Although essentially a vigilante group, the Antis generally maintained a respect for the law and attracted many prominent citizens. By the early 1900's, the group had chapters throughout the mid-west and southwest. In 1916 the Anti-Horse Thief Association had grown to 50,000 members and held a national convention with eleven states represented. In 1928, the name was changed to the Anti-Thief Association. There are still active chapters. *Missouri Historical Review*, July, 1951

81    Koob, Tom, *Enon to Radium Spring*, White Oak Lodge Publishing, 2008, from a  personal interview with Emmett Allen March 11, 2007

82    Rayburn, Otto Ernest, *Forty Years in the Ozarks*, Ozark Guide Press, Eureka Springs, Arkansas, 1957, p.6

83    ibid, p.8

84    ibid. pp.6-7

85    ibid, p.96

86  Randolph, Vance, *The Ozarks, An American Survival of Primitive Society*, edited by Robert Cochran, University of Arkansas Press, 2017, p.7

87  Randolph, Vance and Wilson, George P., *Down in the Holler: A Gallery of Ozark Folk Speech*, University of Oklahoma Press, 1953

88  Randolph, Vance, *Pissing in the Snow & Other Ozark Folktales*, University of Illinois Press, 1976

89  Randolph, Vance, *Roll Me in Your Arms: "Unprintable" Ozark Folksongs and Folklore : Volume I Folk Songs and Music*, ed. Gershon Legman, 1992; Randolph, Vance, *Blow the Candle Out: "Unprintable" Ozark Folksongs and Folklore : Volume II Folk Rhymes and Other Lore*, ed. Gershon Legman, 1992

90  Green, Rayne, in the Introduction to Vance Randolph's *Pissing in the Snow & Other Ozark Folktales*, University of Illinois Press, 1976, p. xv

91  Cochran, Robert, *Vance Randolph An Ozark Life*, University of Illinois Press, 1985, pp.135-140

92  Randolph, Vance, *The Ozarks*, ibid, pp. 271-2

93  Randolph, Vance, "Vance Randolph in the Ozarks", *The Ozarks Mountaineer*, 1981, Introduction, p.3

94  From a personal interview with Vineta (Terherst) Wingate January 23, 2007

95  From a personal interview with Sanford and Arlene Garland February 17, 2007

96  Harkins, Anthony, *Hillbilly A Cultural History of an American Icon*, Oxford University Press, Inc., New York, 2004, p.3

97  McCord, May Kennedy, *Ozark Life Outdoors*, November 1931, p.18 as quoted in Wiley, Robert S., *Dewey Short Orator of the Ozarks*, 1985, p.1

98  Wiley, ibid, p.234

99  From a speech entitled "America, Wither Bound?" made by Dewey Short on April 11, 1938 in Chicago, as quoted in Robert Wiley's *Dewey Short Orator of the Ozarks*, p.222

100  Williamson, Thames, *The Woods Colt*, Harcourt, Brace and Company, New York, 1933, illustrated by Raymond Bishop

101  ibid, p.50

102  Randolph, Vance, *Ozark Mountain Folks*, The Vanguard Press, New York, 1932, p.196

103  Randolph, Vance, *Ozark Folksongs*, Vol. 1., The State Historical Society of Missouri, 1946, pp. 126-139

104  Blevins, Brooks, *Hill Folks A History of Arkansas Ozarkers & Their Image*, The University of North Carolina Press, Chapel Hill, 2002, p.139

105  Green, Archie, "Hillbilly Music: Source and Symbol", from the *Journal of American Folklore*, Vol. 78, 1965, p. 204

106  ibid, p.209

107  ibid, pp,209-10

108   ibid, p.216
109   Bernard, Ryan Carlson, "The Rise and Fall of the Hillbilly Music Genre, A History, 1922-1939." (2007). Electronic Theses and Dissertations. Paper 2059. https://dc.etsu.edu/etd/2059
110   Green, Archie, ibid
111   Hopkinson, Ed, "Dr. Smith's Champion Hoss Hair Pullers", www. encyclopediaofarkansas.net, 2013
112   Green, Archie, ibid, p.222
113   Hay, George D., *A Story of the Grand Ole Opry*, Nashville, 1945, p.37
114   "Hillbilly Heartbeats", *Springfield Missouri News and Leader*, Aug 6, 1933
115   The *Sad Song* also called *The Palace Grand*. May sang this at the home of Dewey Short in Galena when Carl Sandburg came to visit. Sandburg later wrote and asked her to send him the words to "the Sad *Song*." Joan Baez later sang this song and credited May as the source. May recorded it for the Max Hunter collection held at Missouri State University.
116   From a personal interview with May Kennedy McCord's granddaughter Patti McCord McDonald on October 26, 2020
117   Massey, Ellen Gray, *A Candle Within Her Soul Mary Elizabeth Mahnkey and Her Ozarks (1877-1948)*, Bittersweet, Inc., 1996
118   A poem by Mary Elizabeth Mahnkey
119   Mahnkey, Mary Elizabeth, "Service" from Massey, Ellen Gray, "The World of Mary Elizabeth Mahnkey", *Ozarks Watch*, Vol. IV. No.2, Fall 1990
120   Massey, Ellen Gray, *A Candle Within Her Soul*, ibid, p. xv
121   Includes information from a personal interview with Angel Wolf, Mary Elizabeth Mahnkey's great-granddaughter on October 28, 1920
122   Mahnkey, Douglas, *Bright Glowed My Hills*, The School of the Ozarks Press, 1968, p.95-6.
123   Mahnkey. Douglas, ibid, Preface
124   Blevins, Brooks, "The Ozarks Watchers", *Ozarks Watch*, Series 2, Vol. 3, No.1
125   Williamson, J.W., *Hillbillyland*, The University of North Carolina Press, Chapel Hill, 1995, p. 179
126   ibid, pp. 37-8
127   Blevins, Brooks, *Arkansas/Arkansaw How Bear Hunters, Hillbillies and Good Ol' Boys Defined a State*, University of Arkansas Press, 2009, Chapter 3
128   Williamson, *Hillbillyland*, ibid, pp. 42-3
129   ibid, pp. 40-2
130   Blevins, *Arkansas*, ibid, Chapter 3 and Williamson, *Hillbillyland*, ibid
131   From a personal interview with Ermal Phillips May 8, 2007
132   Chapman, Carl H. and Bray, Robert T., "The Culture-Complexes

and Sequence at the Rice Site Stone County, Missouri", The Missouri Archaeologist, Vol. 18, Nos. 1-2, April-July 1956

133    From a personal interview with Wilma (Rice) England and Ann (England) King, May 17, 2007

134    Blevins, *Arkansaw*, ibid, Chapter 3

135    *Christian County Headliner News*, "These millionaires were 'maid' in the Ozarks", March 31, 2016

136    Williamson, *Hillbillyland*, ibid, pp. 53-6

137    Williamson, *Hillbillyland*, ibid, p.8

138    Williamson, *Hillbillyland*, ibid, p.8

139    Leimkuehler, Matthew, *The Tennessean*, 9-14-19, "Is 'hillbilly' an offensive term? Ken Burns' 'Country Music' weighs in"

140    Spears-Stewart, Reta, *Remembering the Ozark Jubilee*, Dillbeck & White Productions, Springfield, Mo., 1993

141    Mueller, Mabel E., "History of the Hillcrofters," Box 13, Folder 8, Center for Ozarks Studies (RG 8.11), Special Collections and Archives Department, Missouri State University, undated

142    Blevins, *Hillfolks A History*, ibid, p. 138

143    Blevins, Brooks, *Ghost of the Ozarks Murder and Memory in the Upland South*, University of Illinois Press, 2012

144    Secrist, William G., "Ozark Murder Reveals System of Peonage", *Kansas City Journal Press*. December 1, 1929, from Blevins, *Ghost*, ibid, p. 35

145    Driftwood, Jimmy, "Music of the Ozarks", LP recording liner notes, National Geographic Society, 1972

146    "Jimmy Driftwood at One Hundred", a presentation by Dr. Brooks Blevins for Talking Ozarks Symposium, Shiloh Museum of Ozark History, 2007

147    From personal interviews with Bob Mabe in 2017

148    Driftwood, Jimmy, *Music of the Ozarks*, ibid

149    Owen, Jim, *Jim Owen's Hillbilly Humor*, Pocket Books, New York, 1970, p. 118

150    From a personal interview with Keith Thurman by Tom Koob March 30, 2021

151    From a personal interview with Keith Thurman by Curtis Copeland July 16, 2020

152    From a personal interview with Josh Heston by Curtis Copeland, January 27, 2021

153    Straub, Peter, *The Nearly Complete Works of Donald Harington,* Vol. 1, Introduction, Lake Union Publishing, 2012

154    From personal interviews with Steve, Beni and Mark Seaton by Tom Koob and Curtis Copeland, April 7 and 27, 2021

155   Randolph, Vance, *The Ozarks A Primitive Society*, ibid, p.271

156   Rayburn, Otto Ernest, "Rayburn's Roadside Chats Arcadian Lore and Logic", Underhill Press, Beebe, Arkansas. 1939, p.3

157   Simon, Charlie May, *Straw In The Sun*, E. P. Dutton & Company, 1945, p.189

158   Perkins, J. Blake, *Dynamics of Defiance: Government Power and Rural Resistance in the Arkansas Ozarks*, Graduate Theses, Dissertations, and Problem Reports, West Virginia University, 2014, p.277

159   Blevins. Brooks, "In the Land of a Million Smiles: Twentieth-Century America Discovers the Arkansas Ozarks", *The Arkansas Historical Quarterly*, Vol. 61. No.1. Spring, 2002 and www.wikipedia.org, "Monte Ne"

160   www.bellavistamuseum.org

161   www.mycherokeevillage.com

162   Koob, Tom, *Enon to Radium Spring*, White Oak Lodge Publishing, 2008, pp. 131-2

163   Catton, Theodore, *Life, Leisure and Hardship Along the Buffalo*, Principal Investigator, National Park Service, 2008, p.246 and Julia McAdoo, "Where the Poor Are Rich", *American Mercury*, 81 (September 1955), p.87

164   ibid. pp.246-7

165   Phillips, Jared M., *Hipbillies, Deep Revolution in the Arkansas Ozarks*, The University of Arkansas Press, 2019, p.136

# Image Credits

Cover (colorized)- Vance Randolph photo collection, Lyons Memorial Library, College of the Ozarks. This photo is notated, "Sam McDaniel, White Rock, Mo. about 1930. He was a member of the Missouri Legislature". According to the *Official Manual of the State of Missouri, Sam* McDaniel was a farmer and lecturer born in 1861. He lived in Pineville, McDonald County and was elected to terms in the Missouri House in 1924 and 1926.

Page 30- Tom Koob

Page 33- Tom Koob

Page 40- Aunt Cassie Wheeler from Townsend Godsey's *Ozark Mountain Folk These Were The Last* with permission of Godsey Photography Foundation

Page 48- Tom Koob

Page 51- Cover of Frederick Gerstaeker's *Wild Sports in the Far West* published in 1859

Page 62- Tommie Redfearn from Townsend Godsey's *Ozark Mountain Folk These Were The Last* with permission of Godsey Photography Foundation

Page 67- Vance Randolph photo collection, Lyons Memorial Library, College of the Ozarks- Randolph titled this photo "To Keep Off Evil Spirits" and gave the following description: "A cedar peg, with three out-thrust prongs, is placed in the pathway to keep witches away from a backwoods cabin. It is said that this device is particularly favored by certain Christian cults, who regard it as representative of the Trinity. It is very bad luck to disturb such a symbol, whether one believes in witchcraft or not. Enlightened hill-people may laugh at these outworn superstitions, but they are nevertheless very careful not to step on a 'witch-peg'"

Page 70- courtesy of the Barry County Museum

Page 80- Cover of C.F.M. Noland's *Cavorting on the Devil's Fork* originally published in 1847

Page 83- an illustration from Thomas Bangs Thorpe's "The Big Bear of Arkansas" originally published in 1841

Page 87- Cover of M. L. Byrn's *The Life and Adventures of an Arkansaw Doctor* originally published in 1851

Page 101- Photo courtesy of Bear Creek Productions, Branson, Missouri, Michael Johnson, Director

Page 103- Vance Randolph photo collection, Lyons Memorial Library, College of the Ozarks. Randolph notates this photo as "still in my backyard". Based on this series of photos taken in the 1930s, it appears that Randolph had the Sheriff set up a captured moonshine still at Randolph's home in Pineville indicating the still may be authentic, but the scene is staged.

Page 108- Leo Drey in the Pioneer Forest courtesy of the L-A-D Foundation

Page 113- Charlie Barnes from Townsend Godsey's *Ozark Mountain Folk These Were The Last* with permission of Godsey Photography Foundation

Page 116 and 117- courtesy of Scotty Chamberlin

Page 120- cover of Wright's *The Shepherd of the Hills* originally published in 1907

Page 132- Vance Randolph photo collection, Lyons Memorial Library, College of the Ozarks

Page 138- courtesy of Sanford Garland

Page 141- with permission of Litho Printers

Page 146- Vance Randolph from Townsend Godsey's *Ozark Mountain Folk These Were The Last* with permission of Godsey Photography Foundation

Page 147- George E. Hall photo. George Edward Hall took photographs of the Ozarks from 1906 to about 1922. He lived in Branson until 1916 when he, his wife Vallie and their only child Lillian moved to Galena. Around 1922, the Halls relocated to Illinois and stopped producing photographs. Hall reproduced many of his original photos into postcards which were sold as souvenirs. The popularity of *The Shepherd of the Hills* by Harold Bell Wright helped promote his photographs of this area. George Hall produced about 1,000 known photos. Many of them do a wonderful job of depicting life and activities in the Ozarks during the early 20$^{th}$ century.

Page 151- "The Hill Billies", copies from Okeh Records Catalog 1925, John Edwards Memorial Collection, Southern Folklife Collection, University of North Carolina

Page 154- Vance Randolph photo collection, Lyons Memorial Library, College of the Ozarks

Page 157- courtesy Angel Wolf

Page 160- with permission of the Ralph Foster Museum Collection, College of the Ozarks

Page 162- with permission of the Museum of American History, Cabot, Arkansas Public Schools

Page 174- courtesy of Ann King

Page 177- *Maid in the Ozarks* playbill

Page 182- Hall photo

Page 192- courtesy of Bob Mabe. Left to right- Jim Mabe, Jon Smith, Lyle Mabe, Bill Mabe, Bob Mabe, Chick Allen, circa 1965

Page 197- promotional map distributed by the White River Booster League

Page 200- Jim Owen courtesy Branson Centennial Museum

Page 208- Seaton "Hillbilly Calendar" image with permission of Multi Printing, Springfield, Mo. Left to right- Mark Seaton, Kenny Lingle, Beni Seaton, Ruth Seaton Thomas, Dorthy Seaton carrying Bruce Seaton, Steve Seaton, Perryleane Lingle, Kevin Lingle, Martha Seaton Wynn, Joe Seaton, Nero the dog. Steve Seaton says that his Dad Bruce is actual lying across a wooden support hidden by his wife Dorthy.

Page 211- Ozark Playgrounds Association promotional brochure

Page 214- Monte Ne postcard

# INDEX